Labor omnia vincit.

©2021 CATHERINE FET · NORTH LANDING BOOKS · ALL RIGHTS RESERVED

SALVĒ

This book of English-to-Latin translation and Latin sentence-building exercises is **a companion** to the *Latin for Kids* textbook. The **Answer Key** pages (pink) are designed to be cut out. Cut them out and stack them in a treasure chest with a high-quality secure lock. Use heavy-duty chains to suspend the chest from the highest tree in your neighborhood and hand the key to your worst enemy until you have finished your translation exercises – neatly hand-written or typed on your computer – and feel you are ready to check the correct answers. I also suggest borrowing a three-headed dog from a neighbor to guard that treasure chest – in order to avoid the temptation to check the correct answers before you are done.

For any new **NOUN** listed at the beginning of a lesson you will find two forms – Nominative case and Genitive case. Next to these forms, you will see *m, f,* or *n* – indicating whether the noun is masculine, feminine, or neuter. In parentheses is the number of the declension. E.g.: ***ars, artis,*** f. (3) – art

For any new **VERB** you will find four forms, or 'principal parts.' These are the forms of the verb that show what conjugation the verb belongs to, and whether it changes its stem across its many forms. The principal parts of the Latin verb *scrībere* – 'to write' – are:
1. *scrībō* – I write (Present tense, 1st person, singular)
2. *scrībere* – to write (infinitive)
3. *scrīpsī* – I have written (Past/Perfect tense, 1st person, singular)
4. *scrīptum* – written (Past Participle, neuter, singular)

In parentheses next to each verb is the number of the conjugation to which this verb belongs.
E.g.: ***scrībō, scrībere, scrīpsī, scrīptum*** (3) – to write

NOUN ENDINGS IN 5 DECLENSIONS

DECL.	1	2		3		4		5
GENDER	F.	M.	N.	M./F.	N.	M.	N.	F.
SINGULAR								
NOM.	- a	- us	- um	- s (modified stem)		- us	- ū	- ēs
GEN.	- ae	- ī	- ī	- is	- is	- ūs	- ūs	- ēī / e
DAT.	- ae	- ō	- ō	- ī	- ī	- uī /ū	=Nom.	- ēī / e
ACC.	- am	- um	=Nom.	- em/im	=Nom.	- um	=Nom.	- em
ABL.	- ā	- ō	- ō	- e/ī	- e/ī	- ū	=Nom.	- ē
VOC.	=Nom.	- e	=Nom.	=Nom.	=Nom.	=Nom.	=Nom.	=Nom.
PLURAL								
NOM.	- ae	- ī	- a	- ēs	- a, - ia	- ūs	- ua	- ēs
GEN.	- ārum	- ōrum	- ōrum	- um/ium	- um/ium	- uum	- uum	- ērum
DAT.	- īs	- īs	- īs	- ibus	- ibus	- ibus/ubus	- ibus/ubus	- ēbus
ACC.	- ās	- ōs	- a	- ēs (- īs)	- a, - ia	- ūs	- ua	- ēs
ABL.	=Dat.	=Dat.		=Dat.		=Dat.		=Dat.
VOC.	=Nom.	=Nom.		=Nom.		=Nom.		=Nom.

VERB ENDINGS

	PRESENT	PAST / PERFECT	PAST / IMPERFECT	FUTURE / IMPERFECT	
				1,2 conj.	3,4 conj.
I	- ō	- ī	- ba-m	- b-ō	- a-m
you	- s	- is-tī	- bā-s	- bi-s	- ē-s
he, she, it	- t	- i-t	- ba-t	- bi-t	- e-t
we	- mus	- i-mus	- bā-mus	- bi-mus	- ē-mus
you pl.	- tis	- is-tis	- bā-tis	- bi-tis	- ē-tis
they	- nt	- ēru-nt (-ēre)	- ba-nt	- bu-nt	- e-nt

he, she, it

	SINGULAR			PLURAL		
	m	*f*	*n*	*m*	*f*	*n*
Nom.	is	ea	id	eī / iī	eae	ea
Gen.	eius	eius	eius	eōrum	eārum	eōrum
Dat.	eī	eī	eī	eīs / iīs	eīs / iīs	eīs / iīs
Acc.	eum	eam	id	eōs	eās	ea
Abl.	eō	eā	eō	eīs / iīs	eīs / iīs	eīs / iīs

I, you

	SINGULAR		PLURAL	
Nom.	egō	tū	nōs	vōs
Gen.	meī	tuī	nostrī	vestrī
Dat.	mihī	tibi	nōbīs	vōbīs
Acc.	mē	tē	nōs	vōs
Abl.	mē	tē	nōbīs	vōbīs

his/her/its own

	SINGULAR			PLURAL		
	m	*f*	*n*	*m*	*f*	*n*
Nom.	suus	sua	suum	suī	suae	sua
Gen.	suī	suae	suī	suōrum	suārum	suōrum
Dat.	suō	suae	suō	suīs	suīs	suīs
Acc.	suum	suam	suum	suōs	suās	sua
Abl.	suō	suā	suō	suīs	suīs	suīs

this

	SINGULAR			PLURAL		
	m	*f*	*n*	*m*	*f*	*n*
Nom.	hic	haec	hoc	hī	hae	haec
Gen.	huius	huius	huius	hōrum	hārum	hōrum
Dat.	huic	huic	huic	hīs	hīs	hīs
Acc.	hunc	hanc	hoc	hōs	hās	haec
Abl.	hōc	hāc	hōc	hīs	hīs	hīs

Lesson I

Nouns:

liber, librī, m. (2) – book
stylus, stylī, m. (2) – stylus, pen
frāter, frātris, m. (3) – brother; plural – *frātrēs*
soror, sorōris, f. (3) – sister; plural – *sorōrēs*
pater, patris, m. (3) – father; plural – *patrēs*
māter, mātris, f. (3) – mother; plural – *mātrēs*
fīlius, fīlī / –iī, m (2) – son
fīlia, fīliae, f. (1) – daughter
vir, virī, m. (2) – man
fēmina, fēminae, f. (1) – woman
dominus, dominī, m. (2) – lord, Mr.
domina, dominae, f. (1) – lady, Mrs.

magister, magistrī, m. (2) – teacher (male)
magistra, magistrae, f. (1) – teacher (female)
amīcus, amīcī, m. (2) – friend (male)
amīca, amīcae, f. (1) – friend (female)
animal, animālis, n. (3) – animal
avīs, avis, f. – bird; (*avēs* – plural)
equus, equī, m. – horse
monstrum, monstrī, n. (2) – monster
piscis, piscis, m. (3) – fish; *pisces* – plural
aqua, aquae, f. (1) – water
vīnum, vīnī, n. (2) – wine
īnsula, īnsulae, f. (1) – island
cibus, cibī, m. (2) – food

nōn – no, not
quid – what (neuter), *quis* – who (masculine), *quae* – who (feminine)
meus – my (masculine), *mea* – my (feminine), *meum* – my (neuter)
tuus – your (masculine), *tua* – your (feminine), *tuum* – your (neuter)

Schola Astronomiae et Rhetoricae (School of Astronomy and Rhetoric) – Latin inscription on a door at the Bodleian Library, Oxford, UK
Salus populi suprema est lex (Safety of the people is the highest law) – Latin inscription on the Southampton Civic Centre (UK), 1932

Translation 1

(*esse* – Present Tense conjugation, singular nouns, questions, responses)

Reminder: In sentences where the subject is a pronoun, like "He is a teacher," Latin drops the pronoun. Instead of *Is magister est*, it's just *Magister est*.

What is this? It's a book.
Who are you? I am a monster.
Who is she? She is my sister.
Is she your mother? No, she is not my mother.
We are brother and sister.
Is it an animal? No, it's not an animal, it's a centaur.
Who is he? My father, Mr. Silvius.
My teacher is Mrs. Flavia.
Is this water? No, it's wine.
Britain (Britannia) is an island.

Make Sentences 1
Animal or not?
Make 7 sentences using the words on this page.
Example: Estne leō animal? Ita, leō est animal.
Is a lion an animal? Yes, a lion is an animal.

Make Sentences 2
Food or not?
Make 7 sentences using the words on this page.
Example: *Suntne bāccae cibus? Ita, bāccae cibus sunt.*
Are berries food? Yes, berries are food.

In the Latin of ancient Rome, whether a vowel was long or short could change the meaning of a word. *mālum* is 'apple', while *malum* is 'evil'

Wow, Mālum bonum!

Translation 2
(singular and plural nouns)

We are girlfriends.
A horse and a bird are friends.
They are sisters.
Are you monsters? No, we are centaurs.
Cats and birds are not friends.
Mothers are teachers.
Father and son are men.
Mother and daughter are women.
Brothers are lords.
Sisters are ladies.

Translation 3
(vocabulary review)

Fathers are brothers.
Sisters are friends (female).
Are these monsters? No, they are horses.
A tablet is not a book.
What is this? This is a temple.
Who is a teacher? I am.
Aemilia is a student, but Flavia is a teacher.
Felix is a friend, and Aemilia is a friend.
What is a sundial? I don't know.
Are these animals? (plural: *animālia*)
Yes, these are snakes.

Translation 4
(singular and plural nouns – with additional vocabulary)

Mark the gender of each noun below, and use the plural form of these nouns in the translation exercise. **Notice** that some masculine nouns belong to the 1st Declension and have *–a* (singular) and *–ae* (plural) endings. For example: *nauta* – sailor, *pīrāta* – pirate, and *agricola* – farmer

LILIUM

stella – star; ***planēta*** – planet; ***regina*** – queen; ***terra*** – land; ***ōceanus*** – ocean; ***rosa*** – rose; ***līlium*** – lilly; ***vīlla*** – villa, house; ***pictūra*** – picture, painting; ***vir*** – man, husband; ***flamma*** – flame; ***herba*** – grass; ***agricola*** – farmer; ***campus*** – field; ***nauta*** – sailor; ***pīrāta*** – pirate; ***inimīcus*** – enemy; ***īnsula*** – island

Stars are not planets.
Queens are not friends.
lands and oceans
roses and lillies
villas and paintings
men and languages

flames and grasses
farmers and fields
Sailors are not pirates.
Pirates are enemies.
Islands are lands.

Mmmm... Cāseus bonus!

Make Sentences 3

Good or bad? Answer the questions using adjectives
bonus – good, *malus* – bad/evil
māgnus – big, *parvus* – small
Latin adjectives usually echo the endings of nouns, for example:
cattus bonus, raeda māgna, ovum parvum

Est monstrum bonum aut malum?
Est oceanus māgnus aut parvus?
Sunt pōma bona aut mala?
Est musca māgna aut parva?
Est sāga bona aut mala?
Est frāgum māgnum aut parvum?
Est pōculum māgnum aut parvum?
Est caseus bonus aut malus?
Est olīva māgna aut parva?
Est pirum māgnum aut parvum?
Est hoc (this) pirum bonum aut malum?
Est haec (this) raeda bona aut mala?

MONSTRUM

PŌMA (FRUIT)

SĀGA (WITCH, FORTUNE-TELLER)

FRĀGUM

MUSCA

PIRUM

Lesson I   Answer Key

In the Answer Key translations I mark long vowels in Latin words.
Start noticing that long vowels always appear in some endings.
For example, in the plural ending *-ī*
magistrī, discipulī, equī

Translation 1   (*esse* – Present Tense conjugation, singular nouns, questions)

Quid est? Liber est.
Quid es? Monstrum sum.
Quae est? Soror mea est.
Estne māter tua? Minime, māter mea nōn est.
Frāter et soror sumus.
Estne animal? Minime, animal nōn est, centaurus est.
Quis est? Pater meus, Dominus Silvius, est.
Magistra mea Domina Flavia est.
Estne aqua? Nōn aqua, vīnum est.
Britannia īnsula est.

Translation 2   (singular and plural nouns)

Amīcae sumus.
Equus et avīs amīcī sunt.
Sorōrēs sunt.
Estisne monstra? Minime vēro. Centaurī sumus.
Cattī et avēs amīcī nōn sunt.
Mātrēs magistrae sunt.
Pater et fīlius virī sunt.
Fīlia et māter fēminae sunt.
Frātrēs dominī sunt.
Sorōrēs dominae sunt.

Translation 3 (Vocabulary review)

Patrēs frātrēs sunt.
Sorōrēs amīcae sunt.
Suntne monstra? Minime, equī sunt.
Tabula nōn est liber.
Quid est? Hoc est templum.
Quis est magister? Sum magister.
Aemilia discipula est, sed Flavia magistra est.
Fēlīx amīcus est, et Aemilia amīca est.
Quid est sōlārium? Nesciō.
Suntne animalia? Ita vērō, serpentēs sunt.

Translation 4 (singular and plural nouns - with additional vocabulary)

Stellae planētae nōn sunt.
Reginae amīcae nōn sunt.
terrae et ōceanī
rosae et līlia
vīllae et pictūrae
virī et linguae
flammae et herbae
agricolae et campī
Nautae pīrātae nōn sunt.
Pīrātae inimīcī sunt.
Insulae terrae sunt.

Lesson II

Verbs

amō, amāre, amāvī, amātum (1) – to love
volō, volāre, volāvī, volātum (1) – to fly
videō, vidēre, vīdī, vīsum (2) – to see
spectō, spectāre, spectāvī, spectātum (1) – to look, to watch
scrībō, scrībere, scrīpsī, scrīptum (3) – to write
habeō, habēre, habuī, habitum (2) – to have
sciō, scīre, scīvī, scītum (4) – to know, to know how
dīcō, dīcere, dīxī, dictum (3) – to say
interrogō, interrogāre, interrogāvī, interrogātum (1) – to ask
respondeō, respondēre, respondī, respōnsum (2) – to respond
habitō, habitāre, habitāvī, habitātum (1) – to live
intellegō, intellegere, intellēxī, intellēctum (3) – to understand

Nouns

carta, cartae, f. (1) – map, sheet of paper
gallīna, gallīnae, f. (1) – hen, chicken
serpēns, serpentis, m. (3) – snake, serpent; plural – *serpentēs*
spectātor, spectātōris, m. (3) – spectator
dea, deae, f. (1) – goddess
fābula, fābulae, f. (1) – story
lapis, lapidis, m. (3) – stone
nōmen, nōminis, n. (3) – name
rēx, rēgis, m. (3) – king
puer, puerī, m. (2) – boy
puella, puellae, f. (1) – girl
līberī, līberōrum, m. pl. – children, kids
urbs, urbis, f. (3) – city; plural – *urbēs*
lingua, linguae, f. (1) – lanaguage
domus, domūs / –ī, f. – house; plural *domūs*
aurum, aurī, n. (2) – gold, money
terra, terrae / –āī, f. (1) – land

Adjectives

bonus – good
malus – bad, evil
vērus – true
albus – white
niger – black
aureus – gold, golden
novus – new
antīquus – old
māgnus – big
parvus – small
stupidus – stupid
intellegēns – intelligent; plural – *intellegentēs* (masculine, feminine), *intellegentia* (neuter)
rīdiculus – funny

Quiz

What is the origin of the word **POLITICS**? Select the correct answer!
A. from the Greek *poly* = 'many' + ticks = blood-sucking bugs
B. from the Greek *politika* = affairs of state

Sonā si Latine loqueris

Honk if you speak Latin

Reminder: Latin nouns are grouped into declensions.
1st Declension nouns end in *–a* (singular) and *–ae* (plural)
magistra – magistrate, domina – dominae
2nd Declension nouns end in *–us, –er, –ir, –r,*
–um (singular) and *–ī, –a* (plural)
magister – magistrī; dominus – dominī, templum – templa
3rd Declension nouns have many different singular endings,
but most of them have the plural ending *–ēs*
Let's review the 3rd Declension nouns we know so far:
pater = father (plural: *patrēs*); *māter* = mother (plural: *mātrēs*); *frāter* = brother (plural: *frātrēs*);
soror = sister (plural: *sorōrēs*); *serpēns* = snake (plural: *serpentēs*); *urbs* = city (plural: *urbēs*);
rēx = king (plural: *rēgēs*); *lapis* = stone (plural: *lapidēs*); *spectātor* = spectator (plural: *spectātōrēs*);
canis = dog (plural: *canēs*)

IOCUS (JOKE)

Why was my dad
so proud that I scored
a 40% on my Latin test?
...Because he always
wanted me to XL.

televisio
(m., Acc. Case – *televisionem*)

Translation 1 (Present Tense verb conjugation)

lectus
(m., Acc. Case – *lectum*)

Reminder: in sentences where the subject is a pronoun,
like "He writes," Latin drops the pronoun.
Instead of *Is scribit*, it's just *Scrībit* = He writes.

I love to fly.
We look, but do not see.
Chickens don't fly.
What do you have?
He loves to write.
What do you (plural) see? We see nothing!
Who knows? I know!
A bird flies. Monsters love to fly.
Spectators look.

pelliculae rīdiculae de cattīs
(funny cat videos)

armārium frigidarium
(m., Acc. Case –
armārium frigidarium)

computatrum
(n., Acc. Case – *computatrum*)

Make Sentences 1   *sella* (f., Acc. Case – *sellam*)

mēnsa (f., Acc. Case – *mēnsam*)

Make 7 sentences using words on this page.
Example: What do you see? I see a dog.
Quid vidēs? Videō canem.

Translation 2   ('to have' using the verb *esse*; personal pronouns)

Reminder: One of the ways to say 'I have' in Latin is to use the verb *esse*. Instead of saying 'I have a pen,' you can say 'Is to me a pen.'
mihī – to me • *tibi* – to you • *eī* – to him/her/it
nōbīs – to us • *vōbīs* – to you (plural) • *eīs* – to them

Reminder: Pronouns *this* and *who/what* in Latin change depending on the gender of the object they refer to.
hoc – this, neuter • *hic* – this, masculine • *haec* – this, feminine
quid – what/who, neuter • *quis* – who, masculine • *quae* – who, feminine

I have a cat.
Do you have a horse?
Yes, I have a white horse. *albus* = white
Do you (plural) have fish (plural). No, we have birds.
We have a good house (*domus, domūs / –ī, f. – house*).
What is your name? My name is... [your Latin name]
He has a golden stone.
They have pens.
Who are you? I am the goddess Diana.
This monster loves to fly.
This story is true.

Make Sentences 2
Make 7 sentences using the words on this page.
E.g.: Do you have a villa? No, I don't have a villa.
Est tibi villa? Minime, nōn est mihī vīlla.

CORŌNA
BACULUM MAGICUM
UMBRĀCULUM
HOROLOGIUM
ĀLAE (wings)
CORŌNA
ŪNICORNIS
Carpe diem! (Seize the day!)
TUNICA   TOGA
CĪVIS RŌMĀNUS (Roman citizen)
VĪLLA
HORTUS

Translation 3 (accusative case singular)

I have a gift for you (*tibi*).
He has a friend.
Do you see the forest?
She holds a pen.
A (male) teacher sees a (male) student.
A (female) teacher sees a (female) student.
I see a temple.
We have a king.
Fish love water.
My friend has an animal.

Make Sentences 3

Make 7 sentences with the words on this page.
Example: What do you have? I have a book.
Quid habēs? Habeō librum.

Etymology – Word Origins

What is the origin of the word **DISASTER**?
dis– is a Latin prefix meaning 'not, wrong, absent,' ***astrum*** = a star in Latin.
disaster = wrong stars = bad situation

pupa (f., Acc. Case – *pupam*)

tabula subrotata (f. Acc. Case – *tabulam subrotatam*)
<< *tabula* = board, *sub* = under, *rotata* = wheeled

pila (f., Acc. Case – *pilam*)

birota (f. Acc. Case – *birotam*)
<< *bi* = two, double, *rota* = wheel

ocularia (n., pl., Acc. Case – *ocularia*)

ānulus (m., Acc. Case – *ānulum*)

monstrum sub lectō (n., Acc. Case – *monstrum*)

Caution is the better part of valor!

Translation 4
(adjectives singular and plural, Nominative case)

The Atlantic Ocean is big. (**Oceanus Atlanticus**)
Your cat is funny.
Rome is an old city. (**Rōma**)
Are monsters stupid? No, they are intelligent.
Forests are big.
Temples are old.
Islands are small.
Cities are new.
Snakes are evil.
What is this? It's a big old stone.

Translation 5
(adjectives and possessive pronouns – singular and plural, Nominative case)

Our mothers are teachers.
Our fathers are lords.
Marcus is a little boy.
Sylvia is a funny girl.
The forest is big, but the house is small.
Your (singular) brothers are good friends.
Is this book new? No, it's old.
Your name is funny.
Your (plural) cat is white.
My (plural) horses are good.
The Latin language is ancient.

Make Sentences 4

Please make sentences – match an object and its quality in Accusative Case.
Example: *Quid vidēs? Video campum māgnum.* What do you see? I see a big field.

Nominative Case	Accusative case: Masculine	Feminine	Neuter
altus – tall, high	*altum*	*altam*	*altum*
aureus – golden, gold	*aureum*	*auream*	*aureum*
caeruleus – blue	*caeruleum*	*caeruleam*	*caeruleum*
viridis – green	*viridem*	*viridem*	*viride*
māgnus – big, great	*māgnum*	*māgnam*	*māgnum*
parvus – small	*parvum*	*parvam*	*parvum*
placidus – calm	*placidum*	*placidam*	*placidum*

CAELUS - CAELUM – SKY
FENESTRA - FENESTRAM - WINDOW
MŌNS - MONTEM - MOUNTAIN
LACUS - LACUM - LAKE
CASTRUM - CASTRUM - CASTLE
CAMPUS - CAMPUM - FIELD
ARBOR - ARBŌREM - TREE

Translation 6
(adjectives and possessive pronouns – singular Accusative case)

I see your new girlfriend.
He/she has a true friend (male).
We love the Latin language.
Kids have a funny cat.
Mr. Silvius has a white horse.
We see a big island!
You (singular) see a black monster.
You (plural) love your land.
Kids love the new teacher.
They see an ancient temple.

Translation 7   (Lesson II vocabulary)

A centaur says: "I am not a horse. I am a human."
Is this woman a teacher? I don't know.
I don't understand your language.
A teacher holds a map and says,
"Here is Europe." (here = *hīc*)
She asks, "Where are the kids?"
He responds that he is an American. (that = *quod*)
The United States is a big land.
We live in Great Britain. (*in Britanniā*)
She lives in a small town. (*in urbe parvā*)
Good gods! Where is my cat?
I know where your cat is. (where = *ubi*)

Etymology – Word Origins
What is the origin of the word **NICE**?
NICE comes from Latin
nescius = ignorant, foolish.
The meaning of **NICE** evolved in English
from "careless, stupid, poor" (13th century)
to "fussy, busy" (14th century)
to "fragile, delicate" (15th century)
to "precise, careful" (16th century)
to "agreeable, delightful" (18th century)
to "kind, thoughtful" (19th century)
Wow!... Nice!

What is the origin of the word **JOURNAL**?
JOURNAL comes from Latin
diurnus = daily << *dies* = day

Sit vis vōbīscum!

How do you say it in Latin?
MAY THE FORCE BE WITH YOU!
Sit vis vobiscum!
vīs, vīs, f. (3) – force • *vobiscum* – with you
sit = *esse* in Subjunctive mood = "may it be"

Make Sentences 6

Make sentences using the verb *doceō, docēre, docuī, doctum* (2) – to teach and the word groups below.

Example: *Avīs docet cattum volare.* A bird teaches a cat to fly.

Singular	Plural
I teach – *doceō*	We teach – *docēmus*
You teach – *docēs*	You teach – *docētis*
He/she/it teaches – *docet*	They teach – *docent*

Who teaches:

magister, magistrī, m. (2) – teacher
mūsicus, mūsicī, m. (2) – musician
āthlēta, āthlētae, m. (1) – athlete
nauta, nautae, m. (1) – sailor
agricola, agricolae, m. (1) – farmer
pictor, pictōris, m. (3) – artist, painter
coquos / -us, coquī, m (2) – cook, chef

Whom they teach:

puella, puellae, f. (1) – girl; Accusative Case – *puellam*
puer, puerī, m. (2) – boy; Accusative Case – *puerum*
discipulus, discipulī, m. (2) – student; Acc. Case – *discipulum*
cattus, cattī, m. (2) – cat; Accusative Case – *cattum*
canis, canis, m. (3) – dog; Accusative Case – *canem*
fīlius suus – his/her son; Accusative Case – *fīlium suum*
fīlia sua – his/her daughter; Accusative Case – *fīliam suam*

What they teach:

pingō, pingere, pīnxī, pictum (3.) – to paint, to draw
scrībō, scrībere, scrīpsī, scrīptum (3) – to write
labōrō, labōrāre, labōrāvī, labōrātum (1) – to work
saltō, saltāre, saltāvī, saltātum (1) – to dance, to jump
cantō, cantāre, cantāvī, cantātum (1) – to sing
currō, currere, cucurrī, cursum (3) – to run
nāvigō, nāvigāre, nāvigāvī, nāvigātum (1) – to sail
coquō, coquere, coxī, coctum (3.) – to cook

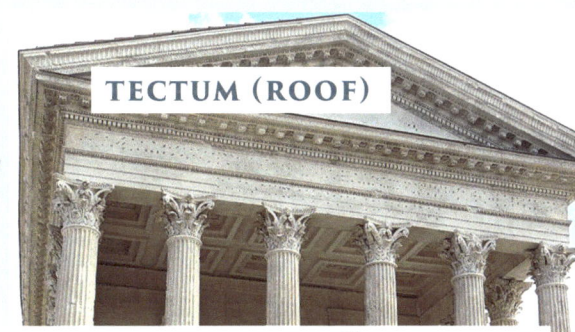

FLŪMEN (RIVER)
LĪTUS (SHORE)
CURSUS FLUVIĪ (THE RIVER'S COURSE)

TEMPLUM
TECTUM (ROOF)
COLUMNAE ORDINIS CORINTHII EX MARMORE FACTA SUNT.
OSTIUM
SCĀLAE (STAIRS)

Make Sentences 5

Make sentences using the verb *dō, dare, dedī, datum* – to give,
personal pronouns *mihī* = to me • *nōbīs* = to us • *tibi* = to you • *vōbīs* = to you (plural),
and the word groups below.

Example: *Vacca dat nōbīs lactem.* A cow gives us milk.

Singular   **Plural**
I give – *dō*   We give – *damus*
You give – *dās*   You give – *datis*
He/she/it gives – *dat*   They give – *dant*

Subject of the sentence:
vacca, vaccae, f. (1) – milk cow
fluvius, fluviī, m. (2) – river
vīnea, vīneae, f. (1) – vineyard
ōceanus, ōceanī, m. (2) – ocean
silva, silvae, f. (1) – forest
campus, campī, m. (2) – field
hortus, hortī, m. (2) – garden
rīvus, rīvī, m. (2) – small stream

Object:
pōmum, pōmī, n (2) – fruit; plural – *pōma;* plural Accusative Case: *pōma*
lāc, lactis, n. (3) – milk; Accusative case: *lactem*
ostrea, ostreae, f. (1) – oyster; plural – *ostreae*; plural Accusative Case: *ostreās*
piscis, piscis, m. (3) – fish; plural – *piscēs*; plural Accusative Case: *piscēs*
grānum, grānī, n. (2) – grain; plural – *grāna*; plural Accusative Case: grāna
fungus, fungī, m. (2) – mushroom; plural – *fungī*; plural Accusative Case – *fungōs*
ūva, ūvae, f. (1) – grape; plural – *ūvae*; plural Accusative Case – *ūvās*
aqua, aquae, f. (1) – water; Accusative Case – aquam
flōs, flōris, m. (3) – flower; plural – *flōrēs*; plural Accusative Case – *flōrēs*

Lesson II   Answer Key

In these Answer Key translations notice the long vowels
that always appear in the following endings:
- the plural ending *-ī* (2nd Declension) ***magistrī, discipulī, equī***
- the plural ending *-ēs* (3rd Declension) ***patrēs, mātrēs, sorōrēs***
- "I" form verb ending *-ō*   ***amō*** = I love; ***videō*** = I see; ***legō*** = I read
- "you" (singular) form verb endings *-ās, -ēs*

amās = you love, ***interrogās*** = you ask, ***vidēs*** = you see

Translation 1   (Present Tense verb conjugation)

Amō volāre.

Spectāmus, sed non vidēmus.

Gallīnae non volant.

Quid habēs?

Amat scrībere.

Quid vidētis? Nihil vidēmus.

Quis scit? Sciō!

Avis volat.

Monstra volāre amant.

Spectātōrēs spectant.

Translation 2   ("to have" using the verb *esse* = to be + pronouns)

Est mihī cattus.

Est tibi equus? Ita vērō, est mihī equus albus.

Sunt vōbīs pisces? Minime. Sunt nōbīs avēs.

Est nōbīs domus bona.

Quod nomen it's tibi? Mihī nōmen est Flavia.

Est eī lapis aureus.

Sunt eīs stylī.

Quae es? Diana dea sum.

Hoc monstrum volāre amat.

Haec fābula vēra est.

Translation 3   (Accusative Case singular)

Habeō dōnum tibi.

Habet amīcum.

Vidēs silvam?

Stylum tenet.

Magister discipulum videt.

Magistra discipulam videt.

Videō templum.

Habēmus regem.

Pisces amant aquam.

Amīcus meus animal habet.

Translation 4
(Adjectives singular and plural, Nominative case)

Oceanus Atlanticus māgnus est.
Cattus tuus rīdiculus est.
Rōma urbs antīqua est.
Suntne monstra stupida?
Minimē, intellegentia sunt.
Silvae māgnae sunt.
Templa antīqua sunt.
Insulae parvae sunt.
Urbēs novae sunt.
Serpentēs malī sunt.
Quid est? Lapis māgnus et antīquus.

Translation 5
(adjectives and possessive pronouns – singular and plural, Nominative case)

Mātrēs nostrae magistrae sunt.
Patrēs nostrī dominī sunt.
Marcus puer parvus est.
Sylvia puella rīdicula est.
Sylva māgna, sed domus parva est.
Frātrēs tuī amīcī bonī sunt.
Estne hic liber novus?
Minimē, antīquus est.
Nōmen tuum rīdiculum est.
Cattus vester albus est.
Equī meī bonī sunt.
Lingua Latīna antīqua est.

Translation 6
(adjectives and possessive pronouns – singular Accusative case)

Videō amīcam tuam novam.
Amīcum vērum habet.
Amāmus linguam Latīnam.
Līberī cattum rīdiculum habent.
Dominus Silvius equum album habet.
Vidēmus īnsulam māgnam!
Vidēs monstrum nigrum.
Amātis terram vestram.
Līberī amant magistrum novum.
Vident templum antīquum.

Translation 7 (Lesson II vocabulary)

Centaurus dīcit:
"Equus nōn sum, homō sum."
Estne haec fēmina magistra? Nesciō.
Linguam tuam nōn intellegō.
Magister cartam tenet et dīcit:
"Hīc est Eurōpa."
Interrogat: "Ubi sunt līberī?"
Respondet quod Americānus est.
America Foederāta terra māgna est.
Habitāmus in Britanniā.
Habitat in urbe parvā.
Dī bonī! Ubi est cattus meus?
Sciō ubi cattus tuus est.

Lesson III

Verbs

dō, dare, dedī, datum (irregular) – to give
legō, legere, lēgī, lēctum (3) – to read
audiō, audīre, audīvī, audītum (4) – to listen, to hear
labōrō, labōrāre, labōrāvī, labōrātum (1) – to work
doceō, docēre, docuī, doctum (2) – to teach
honōrō, honōrāre, honōrāvī, honōrātum (1) – to respect, to honor

Nouns

rēs, reī, f. (5) – thing, matter; plural – *rēs*
rēs pūblica – republic; plural – *rēs pūblicae*; Genitive case singular – *reī pūblicae*
rēx, rēgis, m. (3) – king
rēgīna, rēgīnae, f. (1) – queen
familia, familiās / –ae, f. (1) – family
vīta, vītae, f. (1) – life
campus, campī, m. (2) – field
mundus, mundī, m. (2) – world
pōculum, pōculī, n. (2) – cup, glass
epistula, epistulae, f. (1) – letter, message
hortus, hortī, m. (2) – garden
mōns, montis, m. (3) – mountain
canis, canis, m. (3) – dog
pila, pilae, f. (1) – ball
thēsaurus, thēsaurī, m. (3) – treasure
pīrāta, pīrātae, m. (1) – pirate
sēcrētum, sēcrētī, n. (2) – secret
vēritās, vēritātis, f. (3) – truth
fidēs, fideī, f. (5) – faith
ūniversitās, ūniversitātis, f. (3) – university
mathēmatica, mathēmaticae, f. (1) – math
rēgnum, rēgnī, n. (3) – kingdom

Adjectives

aureus – gold
longus – long
frīgidus – cold

Official state motto of the Caribbean country of Belize is:
Sub umbrā flōreō –
Under the shade I flourish.
flōreō, flōrēre, flōruī (2) – to flourish, to blossom
umbra, umbrae, f. (1) – shade, shadow
sub umbra – Ablative Case

Below: San Pedro in Belize

Translation 1
(Genitive case singular – nouns and pronouns)

This is the new city of the king.
This is the field of our queen.
This is the land of the republic.
I give you (*tibi*) the land of my family.
This is the water of life.
This is the temple of God.
My father's house is big.
The history of Europe is long.
The boy's story is true.
The forests of the world are many.
(many, f. = *multae*)
The water of the ocean is cold.

Make Sentences 1

Make sentences matching the objects and persons to whom they belong. Use words/pictures on this page. Example:
Estne tabula tua? Minime, tabula puellae est.
Is this your tablet? No, it's the girl's tablet.

PECŪNIA
MĪCROSCOPIUM
SACCUS
PRINCIPESSA (princess)
SPECULUM
ĀNNULUS AUREUS
MAGISTRA
MEDICUS
PROFESSOR
MOTOBIROTA

How do you say **COUCH POTATO** in Latin? The potato is native to the Americas. Potatoes were introduced to Europe only in the 16th century. In Ancient Rome there were no potatoes and so no word for 'potato'! To translate 'couch potato' into Latin, we'll use the word *radix* – the same 'root' as in the English word 'radish.'
couch potato = *rādīx lecti*
rādīx, rādīcis, f. (3) – edible root
lectus, lectī, m. (2) – bed, couch

Translation 2 (Genitive case and Accusative case singular – nouns and pronouns)

We are reading the teacher's book.
We ask the girl's father.
I understand the language of my cat.
I know the history of America.
She sees the friend of her daughter.
We love our son's teacher.
I see a temple of a goddess.
They hold a letter of their master.
(their – Genitive case, singular – *suī*)
I love my mother's garden.
They don't understand my friend's story.

Translation 3
(Genitive case and Accusative case singular – nouns and adjectives)

Give me a cup of cold water. (give me = *dā mihī*)
I have the gold cup of my father.
Who understands the ancient language of my homeland?
He reads the new message of the king.
We have a new map of the city.
Do you know the name of the new queen?
The dog loves my brother's white ball.
He sees the great treasure of the pirate.
I know the secret of the black forest.
My daughter's teacher writes a long letter to me (to me = *mihī*)

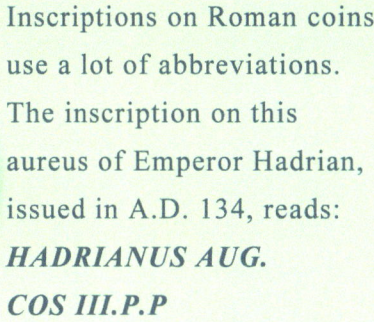

Inscriptions on Roman coins use a lot of abbreviations. The inscription on this aureus of Emperor Hadrian, issued in A.D. 134, reads:
HADRIANUS AUG. COS III.P.P
Aug. = *Augustus*, title of the emperor.
Cos. = *Consul*, the highest office in Senate, usually held by emperor.
III is the number of times the office was held
P.P. = *Pater Patriae* – father of the fatherland, another title given to emperors.

The reverse side of the coin shows a ritual of sacrifice over an altar, and bears the words:
GENIO P.R. – *Genio Populi Romani* = to the genius of the Roman People

On a modern 1-pound British coin the portrait of the queen is surrounded with the Latin inscription: **ELIZABETH II D G REG F D**
D. G. REG. = *Deī Gratiā Regina* – Queen by the Grace of God
F. D. = *Fideī Dēfēnsor* – Defender of the Faith

Translation 4 (Lesson III vocabulary)

Give me the map of the island. (to me = **mihī**)
Listen to the teacher!
I know the truth!
The water of the mountain is silver.
The university professor is writing a long book.
He says this in good faith. this [neuter] = **hoc**
We work on a charitable basis (without pay).
My father teaches math.
The kingdom of the island is small.
I honor the truth.

APIS

The Latin inscription on this gold sovereign of Queen Victoria reads: **VICTORIA·DEI·GRA·BRITT·REGINA·FID·DEF·IND·IMP** = *Victoria Deī Gratiā Brittaniae Regina Fideī Dēfēnsor Indiae Imperātrīx* – Victoria by the grace of God, Queen, defender of the faith, Empress of India

Latin Legal Terms:
Replace the underlined phrase with a Latin legal term:

She has the excuse that she was not at the scene of the crime.
Corrupt politicians offer to exchange favors with technology companies that donate money to their election campaigns.
An examination of the dead body established that the man died of a drug overdose.
Police know this criminal's method of committing crimes.
The law limits the period of time during which a petition demanding explanation for a detention can be filed for state and federal prisoners.
I had to sign some papers for one of my students in place of his parents who were absent.
He suggested this idea without any criminal intent.
Volunteer counsellors work without pay to help kids who use drugs or join a criminal youth gang and end up in a juvenile detention center awaiting trial.

AGNUS

PĀPILIŌ

READING: Latin Mottoes of US States

Alabama	***Audemus Jura Nostra Dēfendere*** – We dare to defend our rights	
Arizona	***Ditat Deus*** – God enriches • ***dītāre*** – to enrich	
Arkansas	***Regnat Populus*** – The people rule • ***rēgnāre*** – to rule	
Maine	***Dirigo*** – I direct • ***dīrigere*** – to direct	
Oklahoma	***Labor Omnia Vincit*** – Labor conquers everything • ***vincere*** – to conquer	

Lesson III Answer Key

In addition to the long vowels in noun and verb endings we studied in the previous lessons, notice the long vowels in the 2nd Declension Genitive Case -ī ending • *magistrī* = of the teacher; *discipulī* = of the student

Translation 1 (Genitive case singular – nouns and pronouns)

Urbs nova rēgis est. Or: Haec est urbs nova rēgis.
Campus rēgīnae nostrae est.
Terra reī pūblicae est. Or: Haec est terra reī pūblicae.
Dō tibi terram familiae meae.
Hoc aqua vītae est.
Hoc templum Deī est.
Domus patris meī māgna est.
Historia Eurōpae longa est.
fābula puerī vēra est.
Sylvae mundi multae sunt.
Aqua ōceanī frīgida est.

Translation 2
(Genitive case and Accusative case singular – nouns and pronouns)

Legimus librum magistri.
Interrogāmus patrem puellae.
Intellegō linguam catti meī.
Sciō historiam Americae.
Videt amīcum fīliae suae.
Amāmus magistrum fīliī meī.
Videō templum deae.
Tenent epistulam dominī suī.
Amō hortum mātris meae.
Nōn intellegunt fābulam amīcī meī.

Translation 3

(Genitive case and Accusative case singular – nouns and adjectives)

Dā mihī pōculum aquae frīgidae.
Habeō pōculum aureum patris meī.
Quis intellegit linguam antīquam patriae meae?
Legit epistulam novam rēgis.
Habēmus cartam novam urbis.
Scīsne nōmen rēgīnae novae?
Canis amat pilam albam frātris meī.
Videt thēsaurum māgnum pīrātae.
Sciō sēcrētum sylvae nigrae.
Magister fīliae meae scrībit mihī epistulam longam.

Translation 4 (Lesson III vocabulary)

Dā mihī cartam īnsulae.
Audīte magistram!
Sciō vēritātem!
Aqua montis aurea est.
Professor ūniversitātis scrībit librum longum.
Hoc dīcit bonā fidē.
Labōrāmus pro bonō.
Pater meus mathēmaticam docet.
Rēgnum īnsulae parvum est.
Honōrō vēritātem.

Lesson IV

ASINUS

Verbs
computō, computāre, computāvī, computātum (1) – to count, to calculate

Nouns
via, viae, f. (1) – road, street
arbor, arbōris, f. (3) – tree; plural – *arbōrēs*
flōs, flōris, m. (3) – flower; plural – *flōrēs*
pānis, pānis, m. (3) – bread
cubiculum, cubiculī, n. (2) – room
caelus, caelī, m. (2) – sky, heaven
stēlla, stēllae, f. (1) – star
sōl, sōlis, m. (3) – sun
arēna, arēnae, f. (1) – sand
mare, maris, n. (3) – sea
occidēns, occidentis, m. (3) – sunset, West
oriēns, orientis, m. (3) – sunrise, East
bōs, bovis, f. (3) – cow
delphīnus, delphīnī, m. (2) – dolphin
ūnicornis, ūnicornis, m. (3) – unicorn
ornāmentum, ornāmentī, n. (2) – ornament;
plural – *ornāmenta* – jewelry
margarīta, margarītae, f. (1) – pearl
pecūnia, pecūniae, f. (1) – money

Adjectives
incōgnitus – unknown
fortis (3rd declension) – brave
fēlīx (3rd declension) – happy
multus – numerous, multiple, many

Monument to the Russian Tsar Peter the Great in St. Petersburg, Russia. The Latin inscription reads:
Petro Primo Catharina Secunda MDCCLXXXII
To Peter the First, by Catherine the Second, 1782
Petro Primo - *Dative Case*
Catharina Secunda - *Ablative Case*

	singular m.	plural m.	singular f.	plural f.	singular n.	plural n.
green	*viridis*	*viridēs*	*viridis*	*viridēs*	*viride*	*viridia*
yellow	*flāvus*	*flāvī*	*flāva*	*flāvae*	*flāvum*	*flāva*
blue	*caeruleus*	*caeruleī*	*caerulea*	*caeruleae*	*caeruleum*	*caerulea*
black	*niger*	*nigrī*	*nigra*	*nigrae*	*nigrum*	*nigra*
white	*albus*	*albī*	*alba*	*albae*	*album*	*alba*
pink	*roseus*	*roseī*	*rosea*	*roseae*	*roseum*	*rosea*
red	*ruber*	*rubrī*	*rubra*	*rubrae*	*rubrum*	*rubra*
purple	*purpūreus*	*purpūreī*	*purpūrea*	*purpūreae*	*purpūreum*	*purpūrea*

Translation 1 (colors)

Trees of the forest are green.
Flowers of the field are yellow.
What color is your friend's dog?
I see a blue room.
The sky is blue and the sun is yellow.
The black mountain is big.
The teacher's kids have a white cat.
I love the blue water and the yellow sand of the island.
The sunrise is pink, but the sunset is red.
A purple cow is funny.

Translation 2 (*in* + Ablative case singular – nouns only)

Fish live in the water.
Where is water? In the ocean.
Birds live in the tree.
Where are trees? In the forest.
Kids live at home.
Where is the house? In the field.
What does he say in the letter?
What does the professor write in the book?
The dolphin lives in the ocean.
A girl sees a unicorn in the garden.

Etymology – Word Origins
What is a **RUBRIC**? A **RUBRIC** is a title, a heading, a section, or a set of directions, especially printed in a different color, like... red!
'Rubric' comes from the Latin *ruber* = red.

READING: More US States' Latin Mottoes

Colorado	***Nil Sine Numine***	– Nothing without providence
	nūmene – Ablative Case of *nūmen* = divine authority	
West Virginia	***Montani Semper Liberi*** •	People of the mountains always free
Missouri	***Salus Populi Suprema Lex Esto*** –	
	The safety of the people shall be the supreme law	

CERVUS

Make Sentences 1

Make sentences matching "who/what" and "where." Example:
Ubi est caseus? Caseus in armāriō frigidariō est.
Where is the cheese? The cheese is in the refrigerator.

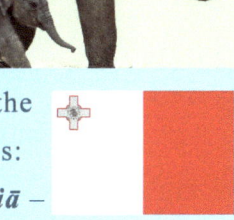

ELEPHANTUS

Who/what:
mīlitēs (soldiers)
lupī
māter et pater
dux (commander)
lapidēs
canis
glīs (dormouse)
aquila
legiō (legion)
convīvium (banquet, feast) • *nūbēs* (clouds) • *caseus*

Where:
castrum – *in castrō*
vīlla – *in vīllā*
mōns – *in monte*
armārium frigidarium (refrigerator) – *in armāriō frigidariō*
caelus – *in caelō*

The state motto of the Republic of Malta is:
Virtūte et cōnstantiā – through strength and consistency
virtūte, cōnstantiā – Ablative Case

Dormice are small rodents. Ancient Romans ate them as appetizers – roasted in honey and poppy seeds.

Treanslation 3
(*in* + Ablative case singluar – nouns and adjectives)

Who lives in the white room?
My friend's daughter.
What is written (*scrīptum est*) on (*in*) the golden tablet?
Wolves live in the big forest.
She writes in the yellow sand.
We live in a small town.
In the black sky there are stars.
This city is on a big island.
The temple is in an unknown land.
Where are the horses? They are in a green field.
Where are the birds? They are in a large tree.

Translation 4
(Dative case singular – nouns and pronouns)

Give us bread.
To a brave man nothing is difficult.
I write a letter to the teacher.
Give the ball to the girl.
I say to my friend: "Thank you!"
I give a flower to my girlfriend.
My friend's father gives his daughter a gift.
She gives water to her horse.
He writes a letter to my sister.
We are reading a book to our son.

LEPUS

Make Sentences 2

Make sentences using the word groups below.
Example: *Dā pānem puerō.*
Give bread to the boy.

to a friend – **amīcō**
cāseus – cheese >>> Acc. Case **cāseum**
arānea – spider >>> Acc. Case **arāneam**
to father – **patrī**
pecūnia – money >>> Acc. Case **pecūniam**
pōculum – a cup >>> Acc. Case **pōculum**
to a teacher – **magistrae**
flos – flower >>> Acc. Case **flōrem**
tabula – tablet >>> Acc. Case **tabulam**

Translation 5
(Dative case – nouns and adjectives)

I give water to a white horse.
Give the ball to the little boy.
We write a letter to a great king.
They give a flower to my good friend.
She says "Hello" to an evil queen.
He gives a cup of water to a student.
We say "Goodbye" to the ancient city.
I write a book for my good friend.
She gives money to a good school.
I am reading a story for a little girl.

In 1910 the British government commissioned Admiralty Arch in memory of Queen Victoria. The Latin inscription on the arch reads: ***ANNO DECIMO EDWARDI SEPTIMI REGIS VICTORIAE REGINAE CIVES GRATISSIMI MDCCCCX*** – In the tenth year of King Edward VII, to Queen Victoria, from most grateful citizens, 1910.

annō decimō – Ablative Case of *annus decimus*
Edwardi Septimi Regis – Genitive case of *Edwardus Septimus Rēx*
Victoriae Reginae – Dative Case of *Victoria Regina*
cives gratissimi – Nominative case

Translation 6 (*velle, nolle*)

I want to read your book.
She wants to see her brother.
We want to study in a good school.
We don't want to live in a big city.
He wants to know the truth.
He wants to say "Hello."
A happy man doesn't want to have money.
I don't want to work on an island.
They don't want to give us gold.
I want to study history.

Translation 7 (Accusative case plural – nouns)

She wants jewelry.
Pirates love pearls.
He loves reading (to read) books.
In the city we see great temples.
I see teachers and students.
We honor our mothers and fathers.
They hold pens.
We are reading stories.
Cats don't like/love dogs.
Cats love fish (plural).

Translation 8 (Accusative case plural – nouns and adjectives)

Give us gold jewelry.
I want large pearls.
I love long books.
Cats love goldfish (plural).
Birds see green trees.

Teachers respect/honor good students.
Cats have funny names.
He has black horses.
This family has country houses
(*vīlla rūstica* = country house)
The queen has many gardens.

Make Sentences 3

Make sentences with the word combinations below.
Example: *Dā mihī flōrēs flāvōs.* Give me yellow flowers.
Dā mihī...

ornāmentum aureum >>> Acc. Case pl. *ornāmenta aurea*
equus niger >>> Acc. Case pl. *equōs nigrōs*
dulce mālum (sweet apple) >>> Acc. Case pl. *dulcia māla*
respōnsum bonum (good answer) >>> Acc. Case pl. *respōnsa bona*
dōnum cārum (expensive gift) >>> Acc. Case pl. *dōna cāra*
nova carta (new map) >>> Acc. Case pl. *novās cartās*
nōmen novum (new name) >>> Acc. Case pl. *nōmina nova*
pictūra pulchra (beautiful painting) >>> Acc. Case pl. *pictūrās pulchrās*
pars māgna (big piece) >>> Acc. Case pl. *partēs māgnās*
locus bonus (good spot/place) >>> Acc. Case pl. *locōs bonōs*

UH-OH...

MUS

Dā mihī partem māgnam!

MMM... DELISH

Translation 9 (Lesson IV vocabulary review)

I can (I know how to) count.

What do you see on the road/in the street?

He has a pen in his hand.

At night (in the night) the sky is black.

There are clouds in the sky. We don't see the stars.

Pink flowers are in the garden.

The gate of the city is white.

True friends know that friendship is a treasure.

(*amīcitia* = friendship)

Studying (to study) at the university is not difficult.

You answer incorrectly.

Dinner is ready. What's for dinner? Fish. (*parāta est* = is ready [feminine])

What is the weather today? It's hot and raining.

The official motto of the city-state of Monaco is: ***Deo juvante*** – With God's help

deo, juvante – Ablative Case

NEW YORK CITY – ***Urbs Novum Eboracum***

The historical seal of the State of New York bears the following inscription in Latin:

Sigillum Civitatis Novi Eboraci

The Seal of the City of New York

Eboracum (later known as York) was a fort and later a city in the Roman province of Britannia. The name *Eboracum* means "the place of the yew trees."

LONDON – *Londinium*

London was founded by the Romans as the fort of Londinium. The name Londinium is likely to have come from the Welsh language and means 'a lake fort.'

PARIS – *Lutetia*

Paris was also founded by the Romans as a military fort. Romans named it ***Lutetia Parisiorum*** – Lutetia of the Parisii. The Parisii were a local Celtic tribe. As to Lutetia, it looks like this ancient Celtic name has one of these three meanings: 'a swamp,' 'dirty,' or 'lots of mice.' Paris in those days was clearly not a glamorous place!

Lesson IV   Answer Key

More long vowels to notice!
- the Ablative Case *-ā* ending (1st Declension)   *in terrā; in aquā*
- the Ablative Case *-ō* ending (2nd Declension)   *in ōceanō, in campō*
- the Dative Case *-ō* ending (2nd Declension)   *amīcō* = to a friend; *Deō* = to God
- the Dative Case *-ī* ending (3rd Declension)

patrī = to the father; *mātrī* = to the mother

- all Accusative Case plural endings:

-ās ending (1st Declension), *-ōs* ending (2nd Declension),
-ēs ending (3rd Declension), *-ūs* ending (4th Declension),
-ēs ending (5th Declension)

magistrōs, lupōs, mātrēs, patrēs, flōrēs, manūs, diēs

Translation 1 (colors)

Arbōrēs sylvae viridēs sunt.
Flōrēs campī flāvī sunt.
Qui color canis amīcī tuī est?
Videō cubiculum caeruleum.
Caelus caeruleus est, et sōl flāvus est.
Mōns niger māgnus est.

Līberī magistrī cattum album habent.
Amō aquam caeruleam et arēnam flāvam īnsulae.
Oriēns roseus, sed occidēns ruber est.
Bōs purpūrea rīdicula est.

Translation 2 (*in* + Ablative case singular – nouns only)

Pisces in aquā habitant.
Ubi est aqua? In marī.
Avēs in arbōre habitant.
Ubi sunt arbōrēs? In sylvā.
Līberī domī habitant.
Ubi est domus? In campō.

Quod dīcit in epistulam?
Quod professor in librō scrībit?
Delphīnus in ōceanō habitat.
Puella ūnicornem in hortō videt.

Translation3 (*in* + Ablative case singluar – nouns and adjectives)

Quis in cubiculō albō habitat? Fīlia amīcae meae.
Quid scrīptum est in tabulā aureā?
Lupī in sylvā māgnā habitant.
Scrībit in arēnā flāvā.
Habitāmus in urbe parvā.
Stēllae sunt in caelō nigrō.
Haec urbs in īnsula māgnā est.
Templum in terrā incōgnitā est .
Ubi sunt equī? In campō viridī sunt.
Ubi sunt avēs? In arbōre māgnā sunt.

Translation 4 (Dative case singular – nouns and pronouns)

Dā nobis pānem.
Virō fortī nihil difficile.
Scrībō epistulam magistrō.
Dā pilam puellae.
Dīcō amīcō meō "Agō tibi grātiās!"
Dō flōrem amīcae meae.
Pater amīcae meae dat dōnum fīliae suae.
Dat aquam equō suō.
Scrībit epistulam sorōrī meae.
Legimus librum fīliō nostrō.

Translation 5 (Dative case – nouns and adjectives)

Dā aquam equō albō.
Dā pilam puerō parvō.
Scrībimus epistulam rēgī māgnō.
Dant flōrem amīcae meae bonae.
Dīcit "Salvē" rēgīnae malae.
Dat pōculum aquae discipulō.
Dīcimus "Valē" urbī antīquae.
Scrībō librum amīcō bonō.
Dat pecūniam scholae bonae.
Legō fābulam puellae parvae.

Translation 6 (*velle, nolle*)

Volō legere librum tuum.
Vult vidēre frātrem suum.
Volumus dīscere in scholā bonā.
Nōlumus in urbe māgnā habitāre.
Vult vēritātem scīre.
Vult "Salvē" dīcere.
Vir fēlīx nōn vult pecūniam habēre.
Nōlō in īnsulā labōrāre.
Nōlunt nōbīs aurum dare.
Volō historiam dīscere.

Translation 7 (Accusative case plural – nouns)

Vult ornāmenta.
Pīrātae amant margarītās.
Amat librōs legere.
In urbe templa māgna vidēmus.
Videō magistrōs et discipulōs.
Honōrāmus mātrēs et patrēs nostrōs.

Tenent stylōs.
Legimus fābulās.
Catti canēs nōn amant.
Catti piscēs amant.

Translation 8 (Accusative case plural – nouns and adjectives)

Dā nōbīs ornāmenta aurea.
Volō margarītās māgnās.
Amō librōs longōs.
Catti piscēs aureōs amant.
Avēs arbōrēs viridēs vident.
Magistrī discipulōs bonōs honōrant.
Catti nōmina rīdicula habent.
Equōs nigrōs habet.
Haec familia vīllas rūsticās habet.
Rēgīna multōs hortōs habet.

Translation 9 (Lesson IV vocabulary review)

Sciō computāre.
Quid vidēs in viā?
Stylum in manū habet.
In nocte caelus niger est.
Nūbēs in caelō sunt. Nōn vidēmus stēllās.
Flōrēs roseī in hortō sunt.
Porta urbis alba est.
Amīcī vērī sciunt quod amīcitia thēsaurus est.
In ūniversitāte dīscere
 nōn difficile est.
Respondēs prāve.
Cēna parāta est. Quid cēnae? Piscis.
Quaenam est tempestās hodiē? Calidum est et pluit.

Lesson V

Verbs
ambulō, ambulāre, ambulāvī, ambulātum (1) – to walk, to travel
lūdō, lūdere, lūsī, lūsum (3) – play
crēdō, crēdere, crēdidī, crēditum (3) – to believe
ēdō, ēdere, ēdidī, ēditum (3) – to eat
cantō, cantāre, cantāvī, cantātum (1) – to sing

Nouns
Rōmānus, Rōmānī, m. (2) – a Roman
imperātor, imperātōris, m. (3) – emperor, commander
mīles, mīlitis, m. (3) – soldier
diēs, diēī, m. (5) – day
parēns, parentis, m., f. (3) – parents
folium, foliī, n. (2) – leaf
lūx, lūcis, f. (3) – light
rīvus, rīvī, m. (2) – stream, small river

Adjectives
magicus – magical
pulcher – beautiful
fortis – brave, strong

A seal ring with an intaglio portrait of Alaric II, King of the Visigoths. Latin inscription reads:
Alaricus, Rex Gothorum –
Alaric, King of the Goths; 5th century AD

Translation 1
(Genitive case plural – nouns and pronouns)

Neptune is the god of the seas and oceans.
Flora is the goddess of flowers.
Mercury is the god of the roads.
Caesar Augustus is the emperor
of the Romans.
This is a gift of my sisters.
He is the king of our lands.
The leaves of the trees are yellow.
This is the history of emperors.
I have a book of stories.
We see the light of the stars.

Translation 2
(Genitive case plural – nouns and adjectives)

I know the names of many of your friends
(your many friends).
A unicorn understands the language of
magical flowers.
This is the history of great kings.
This is a map of small islands.
She is the queen of evil serpents.
He is the king of ancient lands.
Who knows the stories of Roman gods?
Where is the little girls' ball?
I have a book of ancient secrets.
I give you a cup of white pearls.

Translation 3 (*de* + Ablative case singular – nouns, pronouns, and adjectives)

I am reading a story about a king.
This book is about a girl.
My letter is about the truth.
The secret is about gold.
I love stories about life in ancient Europe.
We know about your gift.
Is the letter about your friend?
We are writing a letter about our school.
He speaks about the history of his homeland.
Who knows about the black forest?

Make Sentences 1
Please make sentences matching "what" and "where."
Example: *Ubi sunt equōs? Equōs sunt in campīs.*
Where are the horses? The horses are in the fields.
What: *rosae, piscēs, ornāmenta, poēmata* (poems), *cubicula* (rooms)
Where: *in hortīs, in vīllīs, in ōceanīs,*
in tabernīs (*taberna* = shop), *in librīs*

Translation 5 (Ablative case plural – nouns and adjectives)

Unicorns live in magical forests.
I love walking in ancient gardens.
He writes a letter about Roman cities.
This story is about unknown lands.
A professor writes a book about American forests.
This is a book about ancient secrets.
She speaks about evil hypocrites.
Kids live in small rooms.
Fish live in silver streams.
I am reading a book about brave soldiers.

Translation 4 (Ablative case plural – nouns)

Romans live in villas.
Wolves live in forests.
Flowers and grass are in the fields.
Professors are at (*in*) the universities.
Birds are in the trees.
Maps are in the books.
The book is about Americans.
We read about the cities of the world.
The future is in the stars.
The sun is in the clouds.

PULLUS

The Latin motto on the
seal of the US Department of Justice reads:
Qui pro Domina Justitia sequitur
'who prosecutes on behalf of Lady Justice.'
The original colonial seal read:
Qui pro Domina Regina sequitur
'who prosecutes on behalf of
our Lady, the Queen"

Make Sentences 2 (Dative case plural – nouns)

Make sentences using the word sets below – mix and match!
Example: *Dīcō "Salvē" discipulīs.* I say "Hello" to the students.

What you say:
"Agō vōbīs grātiās!"
"Bene!"
"Quid novī?" (What's new?)
"Nōn intellegō!"
"Quid agitis?"

You say it to:
canibus bonīs
parentibus (*parēns* = parent)
amīcīs
barbarīs
senātōribus

Translation 6 (Dative case plural – nouns)

Give silver to queens.
Give gold to kings.
I read to children.
We say "hello" to the teachers.
They say "goodbye" to the boys.

We don't believe hypocrites.
She believes stories about unicorns.
I believe parents.
Lords believe ladies.
Ladies believe lords.

Translation 7 (Dative case plural – nouns, pronouns, and adjectives)

I believe good friends (male).
She doesn't believe her evil girlfriends.
We give flowers to our beautiful mothers.
We give gifts to our brave sons.
She reads a story to her little daughters.
They give water to their white horses.
He thanks (does thanks to) his good parents.
I give bread to yellow birds.
I believe brave soldiers.
She believes true stories.
Birds sing to/for happy people
(*homo felix* = happy man/human).

The state motto
of the island nation
of Seychelles is:
Finis coronat opus –
The end crowns the work

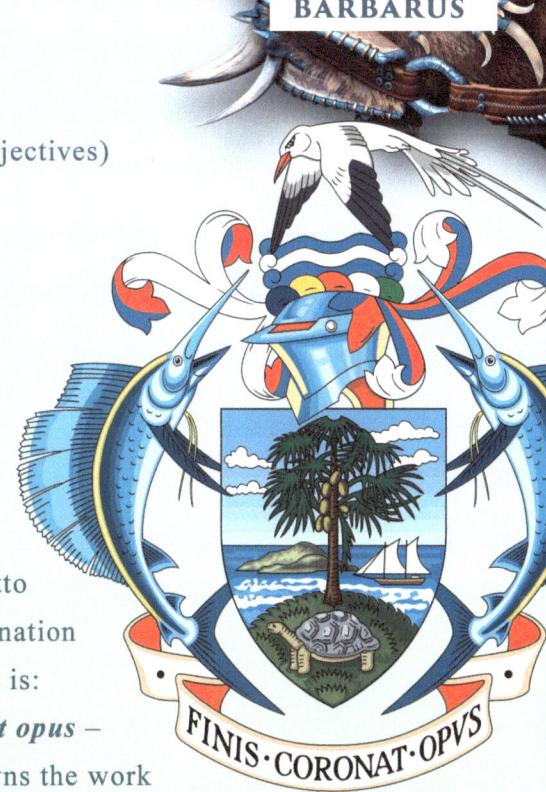

Translation 8 (Vocabulary review)

Kids love stories about animals.
The Latin language is not difficult. It's easy.
I want to study science.
This stone is heavy.
The Glory of kings is short. The Glory of God is forever. (*in saecula saeculōrum*)
I give thanks to the Lord God.
Your dog is lazy.
Kids play, parents work.
Today is my lucky day.
The light of the moon is bright.
We are eating dinner.

READING: *Latin Mottoes of the US States*

Kansas: *Ad Astra per Aspera* – To the stars through difficulties
asperum, asperī, n. (2) – difficult situation; **astrum, astrī,** n. (2) – star
(**ad astra** – Accusative Case, **per Aspera** – Ablative Case)

Oregon: *Alis Volat Propriis* – She flies with her own wings
āla, ālae, f. (1) – wing; **proprius** – one's own;
(**alis, propriis** – 'Instrumental' Ablative Case plural)

Mississippi: *Virtute et Armis* – By valor and arms
(**virtute, armis** – 'Instrumental' Ablative Case)
virtūs, virtūtis, f (3) – manliness, virtue; **arma, armōrum,** n, pl – arms, weapons

South Carolina: *Animis Opibusque Parati* – Prepared with our minds and resources
animus, animī, m. (2) – mind, spirit; **ops, opis, f.** (3) – power, wealth, resources
(**animīs, opibus** – Ablative Case plural)

TĪGRIS

Virginia: *Sic Semper Tyrannis* – This always befalls tyrants
tyrannus, tyrannī, m. (2) – tyrant (**tyrannis** – Dative Case plural)

Lesson V   Answer Key

More long vowels in endings:
• the Genitive Case plural
-ārum ending (1st Declension), *-ōrum* ending (2nd Declension)
rēgīnārum, rosārum, magistrōrum, lupōrum
• the Ablative and Dative cases plural *-īs* ending (1st and 2nd Declension),
rosīs, vīllīs, lupīs, magistrīs, monstrīs

Translation 1 (Genitive case plural – nouns and pronouns)

Neptūnus deus marium et ōceanōrum est.
Flōra dea flōrum est.
Mercurius deus viārum est.
Caesar Augustus imperātor Rōmānōrum est.
Hoc dōnum sorōrum meōrum est.
Rēx terrārum nostrārum est.
Folia arbōrum flāva sunt.
Haec historia imperātōrum est.
Habeō liber fābulārum.
Vidēmus lūx stēllārum.

Translation 2 (Genitive case plural – nouns and adjectives)

Sciō nōmina multōrum amīcōrum tuōrum.
Unicornis intellegit linguam flōrum magicōrum.
Haec est historia rēgum māgnōrum.
Haec est carta īnsulārum parvārum.
Rēgīna serpentum malōrum est.
Rēx terrārum antīquārum est.
Quis scit fābulās deōrum Rōmānōrum?
Ubi est pila puellārum parvārum?
Habeō librum sēcrētōrum antīquōrum.
Dō tibi pōculum margarītārum albārum.

Translation 3 (*de* + Ablative case singular – nouns, pronouns, and adjectives)

Legō fābulam de rēge.
Hic liber est de puellā.
Epistula mea de vēritāte est.
Sēcrētum est de aurō.
Amō fābulās de vītā in Eurōpa antīquā.
Scīmus de dōnō tuō.
Estne epistula de scholā nostrā?
dīcit de historiā patriae suae.
Quis scit de silvā nigrā?

Translation 4 (Ablative case plural – nouns)

Rōmānī in vīllīs habitant.
Lupī in silvīs habitant.
Flōrēs et herba in campīs sunt.
Professōrēs in ūniversitātibus sunt.
Avēs in arbōribus sunt.
Cartae in librīs sunt.
Hic liber de Americānīs est.
Legimus de urbibus mundī.
Futūrum in stēllīs est.
Sōl in nūbibus est.

Translation 5 (Ablative case plural – nouns and adjectives)

Unicornēs in silvīs magicīs habitant.
Amō in hortīs antīquīs ambulāre.
Scrībit epistulam de urbibus Rōmānīs.
Haec fābula de terrīs incōgnitīs est.
Professor librum de silvīs Americānīs scrībit.
Hic liber de sēcrētīs antīquīs est.
Dīcit de hypocritīs malīs.
Līberī in cubiculīs parvīs habitant.
Pisces in rīvīs argenteīs habitant.
Legō librum de mīlitibus fortibus.

Translation 6 (Dative case plural – nouns)

Dā argentum rēgīnīs.
Dā aurum rēgibus.
Legō līberīs.
Dīcimus "Salvē" magistrīs.
Dīcunt "Valē" puerīs.
Nōn crēdimus hypocritīs.
Crēdit fābulīs de ūnicornibus.
Crēdō parentibus.
Dominī crēdunt dominīs.
Dominae crēdunt dominīs.

Translation 7 (Dative case plural – nouns, pronouns, and adjectives)

Crēdō amīcīs bonīs.
Nōn crēdit amīcīs malīs.
Damus flōrēs mātribus pulchrīs nostrīs.
Damus dōna fīliīs fortibus nostrīs.
Legit fābulam fīliābus parvīs suīs.
Dant aquam equīs suīs albīs.
Agit grātiās parentibus suīs bonīs.
Dō pānem avibus flāvīs.
Crēdō mīlitibus fortibus.
Crēdit fābulīs vērīs.
Avēs cantant hominibus fēlīcibus.

Translation 8 (Vocabulary review)

Līberī amant fābulās de animālibus.
Lingua Latina nōn difficilis est. Facilis est.
Volō scientiam dīscere.
Hic lapis gravis est.
Glōria rēgum brevis est. Glōria Dei in saecula saeculōrum est.
Agō grātiās Dominō Deō.
Canis tuus piger est.
Līberī lūdunt, parentēs labōrant.
Hodiē diēs meus faustus est.
Lūx lūnae clāra est.
Cēnam ēdimus.

Lesson VI

Verbs
nārrō, nārrāre, nārrāvī, nārrātum (1) – to tell
parō, parāre, parāvī, parātum (1) – to prepare
veniō, venīre, vēnī, ventum (4) – to come
dormiō, dormīre, dormīvī, dormītum (4) – to sleep
taceō, tacēre, tacuī, tacitum (2) – to be silent
vincō, vincere, vīcī, victum (3) – to conquer, to win

Nouns
silentium, silentiī, n. (2) – silence
fenestra, fenestrae, f. (1) – window
senātus, senātūs, m. (4) – senate

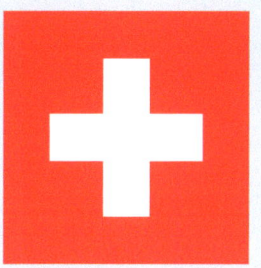

The national motto of Switzerland is:
Unus pro omnibus, omnēs pro ūnō -
One for all, all for one.
omnibus, ūnō – Ablative Case

Make Sentences 1 (*posse*)

Example: *Potes televisionem spectāre?*
Ita, possum televisionem spectāre.

Possum...Nōn possum...
poēmata scrībere
saltāre (to dance)
in nūbibus volāre
cantāre
currere (to run)
cēnam parāre
pingere (to draw, paint)
prōvinciam Rōmānam gubernāre
mathēmaticam docēre

Translation 1 (*posse*)

She can read, but she can't write.
Can you give me water?
Who can prepare dinner?
You can't be everything for everyone
(*omnia omnibus*).
I can't believe stupid people.
We can write a letter to the king.
Eat your dinner and you can play. (*ede* = eat!)
Cats can't fly.
They can tell stories to kids.
Can you see what I see?

The state motto of the South American country of Surinam is: *Justitia, pietas, fides* – Justice, piety, faith

Translation 2
(*ex, cum* + Ablative case singular and plural; – *que*)

I see the ocean from the window.
From the forest the wolf can see the field.
I read with my kids.
She lives with her parents.
We want to walk with our dog.
A bird flies out of a tree.
A boy and a girl play. (Please use -que)
They eat dinner with their friends.
Cats play with dogs.
Birds don't play with cats.

Translation 3
(*in* + Ablative case = location;
in + Accusative case = direction)

Teachers come to school.
They walk in the field.
Students study at school.
Soldiers come to the city.
Birds live in the tree.
A bird flies in the window.
We live in the city.
A lady comes to the temple.
They are at the country house.
A cat sleeps in the street.

Silver Roman dagger found in Germany, 1st century AD

Translation 4 (*ire*)

I am going to the city.
She goes to the forest for a walk (to walk).
They go to their country house.
We go to school.
Are you going home?
Today I am not going to school.
You (plural) go to the temple.
They come and go.
The emperor is going to the senate.

Translation 5
(Verbs – command forms)

Prepare dinner!
Tell me a story!
Go home! (plural)
Come today!
Look and learn!
Read the book! (plural)
Sleep!
Study science! (plural)
Listen and be silent!
Give me water!

Translation 6 (Vocabulary review)

She has the voice of an angel.
Can you go to the city?
We are always ready to play.
If you want to know the truth, read this!
Family is above all.

She wants to see her friend.
Kids are joyful/happy.
The light of the stars is beautiful.
Words are silver, but silence is gold.
Faith always wins.

Lesson VI   Answer Key

Long vowel endings to notice in this lesson:
Command forms of verbs:

1st conjugation command form endings *-ā, -āte*	*amā, amāte, spectā, spectāte*
2nd conjugation command form endings *-ē, -ēte*	*vidē, vidēte*
3rd conjugation command form endings *-ī, -īte*	*dormī, dormīte*
4th conjugation command form endings *-ī, -īte*	*venī, venīte, audī, audīte*

Translation 1 (*posse*)

Potest legere, sed nōn potest scrībere.
Potes mihī aquam dare?
Quis potest cēnam parāre?
Nōn potes omnia omnibus esse.
Nōn possum hominibus stupidīs crēdere.
Epistulam rēgī scrībere possumus.
Ede cēnam tuam et potes lūdere.
Cattī volāre nōn possunt.
Fābulās līberīs nārrāre possunt.
Potes vidēre quod possum vidēre?

Translation 2 (*ex, cum* + Ablative case singular and plural; *- que*)

Videō ōceanum ex fenestrā.
Ex silvā lupus potest campum vidēre.
Legō cum līberīs meīs.
Habitat cum parentibus suīs.
Volumus cum cane nostrō ambulāre.
Avis ex arbōre volat.
Puer puellaque lūdunt.
Cēnam ēdunt cum amcis suīs.
Cattī cum canibus lūdunt.
Avēs cum cattīs nōn lūdunt.

Translation 3 (*in* + Ablative case = location; *in* + Accusative case = direction)

Magistrī ad scholam veniunt.
Ambulant in campō.
Discipulī in scholā dīscunt.
Mīlitēs in urbem veniunt.
Avēs in arbōre habitant.

Avīs volat in fenestram.
In urbe habitāmus.
Domina in templum venit.
In vīllā rūsticā sunt.
Cattus in viā dormit.

Translation 4 (*ire*)

Eō in urbem.
In silvam ambulāre it.
In vīllam rūsticam suam eunt.
In scholam īmus.
Is domum?

Hodiē in scholam nōn eō.
In templum ītis.
Veniunt et eunt.
Imperātor in senātum it.

Translation 5 (Verbs – command forms)

Parā cēnam!
Nārrā mihī fābulam!
Ite domum!
Venī hodiē!
Spectā et dīsce!

Librum legite!
Dormī!
Dīscite scientiam!
Audī et tacē!
Dā mihī aquam!

Translation 6 (Vocabulary review)

Vōx angelī habet.
Potes in urbem īre?
Sumus semper parātī lūdere.
Si vīs vēritātem scīre, lege hoc!
Familia suprā omnia est.

Vult amicum vidēre.
Līberī laetī sunt.
Lūx stēllārum pulchra est.
Verba argentum sunt,
sed silentium aurum est.
Fidēs semper vincit.

Lesson VII

Verbs
putō, putāre, putāvī, putātum (1) – to think
absum, abesse, āfuī, abfutūrum (irregular) – to be absent
adsum, adesse, adfuī / affuī, adfutūrum (irrregular) – to be present
abeō, abīre, abiī / abivī, abitum (irrregular) – to leave
adeō, adīre, adiī / adivī, aditum (irregular) – to approach, to visit
adveniō, advenīre, advēnī, adventum (4) – to arrive, to reach
capiō, capere, cēpī, captum (3) – to catch, to seize

Adjectives
trīstis – sad
Rōmānus – Roman

RĀNA

Nouns
victōria, victōriae, f. (1) – victory
initium, initiī, n. (2) – beginning
fīnis, fīnis, m. (3) – end, boundary
lībertās, lībertātis, f. (3) – freedom
labor, labōris, m. (3) – work
fortūna, fortūnae, f. (2) – fortune, wealth, prosperity
continēns, continentis, f. (3) – continent
cētus, cētī, m. (2) – whale
nūntium, nūntiī, n. (2) – news, message
servus, servī, m. (2) – servant, slave
cīvis, cīvis, m. (3) – citizen

mare, maris, n. (3) – sea

Nom.	mare	maria
Gen.	maris	marium
Dat.	marī	maribus
Acc.	mare	maria
Abl.	marī	maribus

Make Sentences 1 (preposition *ad*)
Match who goes where. Example:
Mīles ad castrum it. A soldier goes to the fort.

Who: *senātor, imperātor, puella parva, mīlitēs, rēgīna, lupus*
Where: *palātium (palace) – ad palātium; urbs – ad urbem; silva – ad silvam; forum – ad forum; campus – ad campum schola – ad scholam; vīlla – ad vīllam*

Latin inscription on the ceiling of the Butler Library, Columbia University, New York:
Homines dum docent discunt – Men learn while they teach. (from the seventh letter of Seneca the Younger, 4 BC – 65 AD).

Translation 1 (prepositions *ā/ab, ad*)

Isn't he coming from the city?
I read books from the beginning to the end.
Science comes from freedom.
Prosperity/wealth comes from work.
Birds fly from continent to continent.
Whales go from ocean to ocean.
News goes from land to land.
We go from victory to victory.
This is my land, from the forest to the sea.
I am learning Latin from my father.

The Latin found on a US dollar bill

Annuit coeptis – 'approves of our undertakings'
Combined with the 'eye of Providence' and the date **MDCCLXXVI** = 1776,
the meaning of **Annuit coeptis** is: God favors the creation of the United States and its undertakings.
annuō, annuere, annuī, annūtum (3) – to nod, to agree
coeptum – beginning, undertaking (from *coepī, coepisse, coepī, coeptum* (3) – to begin)
coeptis – Dative Case plural
The phrase **annuit coeptis** is borrowed from the *Aeneid* – the epic poem by the Roman poet Virgil.

Novus ordo seclorum – new order of the ages; *ōrdō, ōrdinis,* m. (3) – order
sēculum, sēculī, n. (3) – age;   *sēculōrum* – Genitive Case plural
This phrase comes from the fourth *Eclogue* of Virgil,
a poem composed in the poetic meter
of hexameter. To make the word *sēculōrum*
fit into hexameter, Virgil dropped the letter *u*
sēculōrum >> *sēclōrum*

E pluribus unum – 'from many, one' – is a reference
to the union formed by the 13 original colonies
plūribus is Ablative Case plural of *plus* – 'more' – comparative degree of *multus*

Translation 2 (prefixes *a-/ab-*, *ad-*)

Where are my students? They are absent!
Come/approach and see my treasure!
We arrive (***advenire***) in Europe.
My dad is away, but my mom is here (is present).
His brother is away, but his sister is here.
The wolves are near (are present).
Cicero is present at the senate, but Cesar is absent. (***in senātū***)
I am here [present] and I hear you.
We are away, but we are with you in spirit. (***in spīritū***)
Cats are here [present], but the birds are away [absent].
The king arrives (***advenire***) today.

Sundial inscription:
Hōrās nōn numerō nisi serēnās –
I don't count hours unless
it's good weather.
(When it's cloudy a sundial
doesn't work!)

Translation 3 (*quālis/quāle/quālēs/quālia; quālis...tālis*)

What kind of a land is Italy? (***Italia***)
It's a peninsula (***pēnīnsula***).
Like mother, like daughter.
What is this old road like?
What kinds of temples are there in Rome?
(***Rōmae*** = in Rome)

What kinds of birds live in Germany? (***Germānia***)
What kinds of people live in your town?
Like master, like servant.
What kind of letter are you writing?
What kinds of friends do you have?
What kind of land do you see?

Translation 4 (*Accusativus cum infinitivo* – nouns, singular)

She sees her brother sleep.
We see a bird fly.
They hear a bird sing.
I think my sister is sad. (I think my sister to be sad.)
I know that he is a good man. (I know him to be a good man.)
See a cat eat a fish?
He says he is a soldier. (He says himself to be a soldier.)
I want my friend to be here (be present).
Do you hear the teacher read/reading?
Want me to play with you?

Sundial inscription:
Sōl lūcet omnibus –
The sun shines for
everyone. ***omnibus*** –
Dative Case plural

Translation 5 (*Accusativus cum infinitivo* – nouns and adjectives, singular)

Who thinks my country house is small?
I think the brave man always wins.
He sees a black dog catch the ball.
I think my sister is a beautiful woman.
I hear a joyful voice sing.
She knows that the evil queen is away (is absent).
We want our little sister to live with us.
They don't want the new teacher to be angry.
Do you think your new friend knows this?
I want my new student to study astronomy.

A vintage exlibris:
Ad altiora tendo –
I reach for the higher [principles, ideas]
tendō, tendere, tetendī, tentum (3) –
to reach; *altiōra* – neuter plural,
Accusative Case of *altius* =
comparative degree of *altus* = high

Translation 6 (*Accusativus cum infinitivo* – nouns and adjectives, plural)

I see the white birds fly.
We hear the little girls play.
They think black cats are funny.
We know that ancient temples are beautiful.
He sees many people walking in the street.
He wants the Roman soldiers to win.
I see the white horses eat grass.
They see many soldiers go to the city.
I know that Roman citizens are brave.
They hear kids sing.

A vintage exlibris:
Industria et Persēverantia –
Diligence and perseverance

Translation 7 (Vocabulary review)

Roman soldiers are at the gates.
I am tired. Why are you tired?
He is not lazy. He works from sunrise
to sunset (*ab oriente ad occidente*).
The cat is looking out the window.
I ask her, but she is silent.
Show me your new book.
Our king can destroy your city.
I am reading the first page, you read the second page.
Why is your sister crying?
The unicorn sleeps under the black trees.

Lesson VII   Answer Key

Long vowels to notice in this lesson:
Many Latin prepositions come from the Ablative Case forms of adjectives, and so they have the Ablative Case long-vowel *-ā* endings. They include the prepositions *extrā* = outside of, *intrā* = inside of, *īnfrā* = below, *suprā* = above, *iūxtā* = near, *citrā* = this side, *ultrā* = on the further side, *ontrā* = against
Prepositions *ā* = from, and *ē* = out of are also long vowels.

Translation 1 (prepositions *ā/ab, ad*)

Venitne ab urbe?
Legō librōs ab initiō ad fīnem.
Scientia ā lībertāte venit.
Fortūna ā labōre venit.
Avēs ā continente ad continentem volant.
Cētī ab ōceanō ad ōceanum eunt.
Nūntium a terrā ad terram it.
Imus ā victōriā ad victōriam.
Haec est terra mea, ā silvā ad mare.
Dīscō linguam Latinam ā patre meō.

Translation 2 (prefixes *a-/ab-, ad-*)

Ubi sunt discipulī meī? Absunt!
Adīte et vidēte thēsaurum meum.
Advenīmus in Eurōpam.
Pater meus abest, sed māter mea adest.
Frāter suus abit, sed soror sua adest.
Lupī adsunt.
Cicerō in senātū adest, sed Caesar abest.
Adsum et te audiō.
Absumus, sed tecum in spīritū sumus.
Catti adsunt, sed avēs absunt.
Rēx advenit hodiē.

Translation 3

(*quālis/quāle/quālēs/quālia; quālis...tālis*)

Quālis terra Italia est? Pēnīnsula est.
Quālis māter, tālis fīlia.
Quālis haec via antīqua?
Quālia templa Rōmae sunt?
Quālēs avēs in Germāniā habitant?
Quālēs hominēs in urbe tuā habitant?
Quālis dominus, tālis servus.
Quālem epistulam scrībis?
Quālēs amīcōs habēs?
Quālem terram vidēs?

Translation 4

(*Accusativus cum infinitivo* – nouns, singular)

Videt frātrem suum dormīre.
Vidēmus avem volāre.
Audiunt avem cantāre.
Putō sorōrem meam trīstem esse.
Sciō eum virum bonum esse.
Vidēs cattum piscem edere?
Dicit sē mīlitem esse.
Volō amīcum meum adesse.
Audīs magistrum legere?
Vīs mē tēcum lūdere?

Translation 5
(*Accusativus cum infinitivo* – nouns and adjectives, singular)

Quis putat vīllam meam rūsticam parvam esse?
Putō virum fortem semper vincere.
Videt canem nigrum pilam capere.
Putō sorōrem meam fēminam pulchram esse.
Audiō vōcem laetam cantāre.
Scit rēgīnam malam abesse.
Volumus sorōrem parvam nostram nōbīscum habitare.
Nōlunt magistrum novum īrātum esse.
Putās amīcum novum tuum hoc scīre?
Volō discipulum novum meum astronomiam dīscere.

Translation 6
(*Accusativus cum infinitivo* – nouns and adjectives, plural)

Videō avēs albās volare.
Audīmus puellās parvās lūdere.
Putant cattōs nigrōs rīdiculōs esse.
Scīmus templa antīqua pulchra esse.
Videt multōs hominēs in viā ambulāre.
Vult mīlitēs Rōmānōs vincere.
Videō equōs albōs herbam edere.
Vident multōs mīlitēs in urbem īre.
Sciō cīvēs Rōmānōs fortēs esse.
Audiunt līberōs cantāre.

Translation 7 (Vocabulary review)

Mīlitēs Rōmānī ad portās sunt.
Fessus sum. Cūr fessus es?
Nōn piger est. Labōrat ab oriente ad occidente.
Cattus ex fenestrā spectat.
Interrogō eam, sed tacet.
Ostende mihī librum tuum novum.
Rēx noster urbem tuam dēlēre potest.
Legō pāginam prīmam, legis pāginam secundam.
Cūr soror tua plōrat?
Unicornis sub arbōrēs nigrās dormit.

Lesson VIII

Verbs
expectō, expectāre, expectāvī, expectātum (1) – to expect
lūceō, lūcēre, lūxī (2) – to shine
līberō, līberāre, līberāvī, līberātum (1) – to free, to liberate
perdō, perdere, perdidī, perditum (3) – to lose
pulsō, pulsāre, pulsāvī, pulsātum (1) – to hit, to beat, to pulsate
inveniō, invenīre, invēnī, inventum (4) – to find, to discover
vocō, vocāre, vocāvī, vocātum (1) – to call, to summon
rīdeō, rīdēre, rīsī, rīsum (2) – to laugh, to ridicule
salūtō, salūtāre, salūtāvī, salūtātum (1) – to greet
sūmō, sūmere, sūmpsī, sūmptum (3) – to take
fluō, fluere, flūxī, flūxum (3) – to flow
currō, currere, cucurrī, cursum (3) – to run
sedeō, sedēre, sēdī, sessum (2) – to sit
stō, stāre, stetī, statum (1) – to stand

Nouns
ecclēsia, ecclēsiae, f. (1) – church
theātrum, theātrī, n. (2) – theater
verbum, verbī, n. (2) – word
pastor, pastōris, m (3) – shepherd
idea, ideae, f. (1) – idea
fulmen, fulminis, n. (3) – lightning
fluvius, fluviī, m. (3) – river
sella, sellae, f. (1) – chair
clāvis, clāvis, f. (3) – key
forum, forī, n. (2) – square, forum

Adjectives
ingeniōsus – talented
brevis (3rd declension) – short
frīgidus – cold

Adverbs:
herī – yesterday
saepe – often
procul – far

Sundial inscription:
Cito praeterit aetas –
Life goes fast
aetās, aetātis, f. (3) – life, age
praeterīre – to pass by

The motto of Bermuda is:
Quo fata ferunt – Wherever the fates carry us
fātum, fātī, n. (2) – destiny, fate
ferō, ferre, tulī, lātum (irregular) – to carry

Make Sentences 1 (Past Imperfect tense – *esse, abesse, adesse*)

Make sentences using antonyms. Example:
Herī trīstis eram. Hodiē laetus sum. Yesterday I was sad. Today I am joyful.

Yesterday: *lentus* (slow), *parvus, fessus* (tired), *miser, servus, īrātus* (angry)
Today: *fēlīx, fortis, celer* (fast), *rēx / rēgīna, māgnus, benīgnus* (friendly)

Translation 1 (Past Imperfect tense – *esse, abesse, adesse*)

Verbs formed from *esse* – such as *adesse* = to be near, to be present and
abesse = to be away, to be absent – change their forms exactly like *esse*.
For example: *eram* = I was; *aberam* = I was away; *aderam* = I was present

I was and I am a good student.
My father was a Roman citizen.
Where were you (plural) yesterday?
We were present.
Kids were joyful.

My brother and my sister were away.
The sea was blue. The sun was bright.
You (singular) were in the city.
Who was present in church? *(in ecclēsiā)*
The emperor and his son were present at the theater. *(in theātrō)*

Make Sentences 2 (Past Imperfect tense)

Make sentences using the verbs: *vidēre* – to see; *vidēbam* – I saw
legere – to read; *legēbam* – I read
Example: *Herī legēbam ācta diurna. Hodiē legō librum.*
Yesterday I read a newspaper. Today I read a book.
What you read and what you see:
epistulae amīcōrum; hamaxostichus (train);
liber de historiā Iaponiae (a book about the history of Japan)
ācta diurna (newspaper – neuter, always plural)
fabulae frātrum Grimm; ōrātiōnēs Cicerōnis (*ōrātiō* = speech)
mōns ignifer (volcano; Acc. case: *montem igniferum*)
aeroplanum; *Mare Mediterraneum*
(Acc. case: *Mare Mediterraneum*); *Londinium* (London)

FŪMUS
ĪGNIS
CRĀTĒR
MŌNS IGNIFER

Translation 2 (Past Imperfect tense)

Monstrum in pōtiōne Arabicā! (coffee)

Reminder: To form the Past Imperfect tense, remove *-re* from the infinitive form of the verb and add the Past Imperfect tense ending. For example:

amāre >> amā >> amābam • vidēre >> vidē >> vidēbam

Important! If the verb belongs to the 4th Conjugation, add an *-e* before adding the Past Imperfect endings:

audīre >> audiēbam = I was listening / hearing
venīre >> veniēbam = I used to come / I was coming
dormīre >> dormiēbam = I was sleeping

For the following translation I will provide the infinitive form of each verb.

I always expected to see my friends. << *expectāre*
She always read the first page. << *legere*
We were writing letters to the teacher. << *scrībere*
They always showed me their paintings. << *ostendere*
You slept well. << *dormīre bene*
Who was listening? << *audīre* Nobody! (*nēmō* = nobody)
He believed the queen. << *crēdere*
You (plural) loved to walk in the forest. << *amāre*
Kids played. We watched. << *lūdere, spectāre*
She told me stories. << *nārrāre*

Arānea in gelātō!

Make sentences 3 (Past Imperfect tense)

Make sentences using the verbs *venīre* and *vidēre* + the word groups below.
Example: *Vēnī ad montem. Vīdī aquilam.* I came to the mountain. I saw an eagle.

Where you came: *domum* – home; *ad ōceanum Atlanticum; Romam* – to Rome
ad Londinium – to London; *ad montem igniferum* (*mōns ignifer* = volcano)
ad meam vīllam rusticam; ad bibliothēcam – to the library
What you saw: *flūmen Tamesis* (the River Thames); *monstrum sub lectō; templa māgnifica;*
flūmen Tiberis (the Tiber River); *liber de historiā vampyrōrum* (a book about the history of vampires); *squālus* = shark; *īgnis et fūmus* (Accusative case *īgnem et fūmum*);
arānea in mūrō = a spider on the wall

Translation 3 (Past Perfect tense)

Reminder: Verbs usually change their stem in the Past Perfect tense. Dictionaries (and this book) always list the Past Perfect "I" form of verbs as one of the Principal Parts. For example: **nārrō, nārrāre, nārrāvī, nārrātum** (1) – to tell

The Past Perfect "I" form is **nārrāvī**. The Past Perfect stem is **nārrāv-**.

To make Past Perfect forms add these Past Perfect endings to the stem:

Singular	Plural
-i	-imus
-isti	-istis
-it	-erunt

LOCUSTA

For the following translation I will provide the Past Perfect "I" form of each verb.

The king has liberated his land. << *līberāvī*
She has told the truth. << *dīxī*
Caesar came, saw, and conquered. << *vēnī, vīdī, vīcī*
They have lost my book. << *perdidī*
You hit him. << *pulsāvī*
Columbus discovered America. << *invēnī*
Who has called me? << *vocāvī*
He laughed and went home. << *rīsī, īvit* = he went
Your sister greeted me. << *salūtāvī*
Our friends gave us gold. << *dedī*

IOCUS (joke)

- *Cur non reddidisti anulum quem tu invenisti?*
(Why didn't you return the ring you found?)
- *Non putavi esse necesse.* (I didn't think it was necessary.)
- *Quomodo?* (Why?)
- *In anulo scriptum est: 'Tuus in aeternum.'*
(On the ring it is written: 'Yours for eternity.')

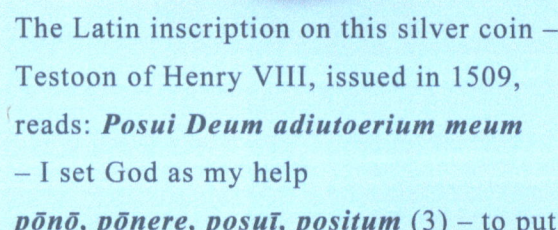

The Latin inscription on this silver coin – Testoon of Henry VIII, issued in 1509, reads: **Posui Deum adiutoerium meum** – I set God as my help

pōnō, pōnere, posuī, positum (3) – to put

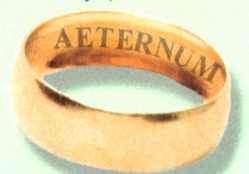

An aureus of Emperor Trajan reads: **IMP CAES NERVA TRAIAN AVG GERM** *Imperator Caesar Nerva Trajan Augustus Germanicus* – *Germanicus* is an honorary title commemorating military victories in Germania.

Translation 4 (Past Perfect and Past Imperfect tenses 1)

Choose the correct form of the verb – Perfect or Imperfect.

We always respected talented teachers. *(honōrābāmus / honōrāvimus)*
Who took my money? *(sūmēbat / sūmpsit)*
Why was she crying? *(plōrābat / plōrāvit)*
They said that I was / am lazy! *(dīcēbant / dīxērunt)*
I gave the ball to the kids. *(dabam / dedī)*
A stream ran / flowed in the woods. *(fluēbat / flūxit)*
The shepherds caught a wolf. *(capiēbant / cēpērunt)*
A cat ate a fish. *(edēbat / ēdit)*
They often came to the theater. *(veniēbant / vēnērunt)*
He came home yesterday. *(veniēbat / vēnit)*

The motto of the British Virgin Islands is:
Vigilāte – Be watchful
vigilō, vigilāre, vigilāvī, vigilātum (1) – to be awake

Translation 5 (Past Perfect and Past Imperfect tenses 2)

Her homeland was far away.
Why were you sad?
The road was short.
Who came first?
I saw your friend in church.

The horses were running in the field. *(currēbant / cucurrērunt)*
The bad ideas didn't win. *(vincēbant / vīcērunt)*
I was thinking about you. *(putābam / putāvī)*
We saw lightning.
The river was cold.

'Dessert' in Latin is
mensa secunda – 'the second meal'

The motto of the British territory of Gibraltar is:
Nulli expugnabilis hosti – Conquered by no enemy
expūgnābilis – conquered
hostis, hostis, m.,f. (3) – enemy
nūllī hostī – Dative Case

VULPĒS

Translation 6 (Vocabulary review)

Who has seen him?
This cat is ill-behaved.
She sits in a chair.
I want to discover unknown lands.
We have lost the key.
It was night, and the sky was black.
The soldiers are standing in the square.
He lost faith.
I love Ancient Rome and Ancient Greece.
They gave us a splendid gift.

Roman Military Commands
Parātī – Get ready
Movē – Forward
Percute – Charge
Stā – Halt
Mūtā locum – Change position
Ordinem servāte – Maintain the formation
Nemo demittat – Nobody break ranks
Silentium – Silence
Nemo antecedat bandum – Nobody advance ahead of the banner
Adiuta Deus – God help us

The motto of Puerto Rico is:
Joannes est nomen ejus – John is his name. It comes from the Gospel of Luke 1:63, reminding us that originally the island was named "San Juan" in honour of Saint John the Baptist. • *eius* – Genitive Case of *is* – he

The motto of the island of Sicily is:
Animus Tuus Dominus (often contracted to "ANTUDO") – Courage is your lord.
animus, animī, m. (2) – mind, character, courage

The motto of the medieval city-state of Florence was:
Regna cadunt luxu, surgunt virtutibus urbes! Kingdoms fall through luxury, cities rise through virtues.
cadō, cadere, cecidī, cāsum (3) – to fall
surgō, surgere, surrēxī, surrēctum (3) – to rise
luxus, luxūs, m. (4) – luxury
virtūs, virtūtis, f. (3) – virtue
luxū, virtūtibus – Ablative Case

Dēpōne dextra/sinistra – Turn right/left
Ad latus stringe – Close the ranks

Lesson VIII   Answer Key

Translation 1 (Past Imperfect tense – *esse, abesse, adesse*)

Eram et sum discipulus bonus.   *Frāter meus et soror mea aberant.*
Pater meus cīvis Rōmānus erat.   *Mare caeruleum erat, et sōl clārus erat.*
Ubī erātis herī?   *Tu erās in urbe.*
Aderāmus.   *Quis in ecclēsiā aderat?*
Līberī laetī erant.   *Imperātor et fīlius suus in theātrō aderant.*

Translation 2 (Past Imperfect tense)

Semper expectābam amīcōs meōs vidēre.   *Quis audiēbat? Nēmō!*
Semper legēbat pāginam prīmam.   *Crēdēbat rēgīnae.*
Scrībēbāmus epistulās magistrō.   *Amābātis in silvā ambulāre.*
Semper ostendēbant mihī pictūrās suās. *Līberī lūdēbant. Spectābāmus.*
Dormiēbās bene.   *Fābulās mihī nārrābat.*

Translation 3 (Past Perfect tense)

Rēx terram suam līberāvit.
Vēritātem dīxit.
Caesar vēnit, vīdit, vīcit.
Perdidērunt librum meum.
Pulsāvistī eum.
Columbus Americam invēnit.
Quis mē vocāvit?
Rīsit et domum īvit.
Soror tua mē salūtāvit.
Amīcī nostrī aurum nōbīs dedērunt.

Translation 4 (Past Perfect and Past Imperfect tenses 1)

Semper honōrābāmus magistrōs ingeniōsōs.
Quis pecūniam meam sūmpsit?
Cūr plōrābat?
Dīxērunt quod piger sum.
Dedī pilam līberīs.
Rīvus fluēbat in silvīs.
Pastōrēs lupum cēpērunt.
Cattus piscem ēdit.
Saepe in theātrum veniēbant.
Vēnit domum herī.

Translation 5 (Past Perfect and Past Imperfect tenses 2)

Patria sua procul erat.
Cūr trīstis erās?
Via brevis erat.
Quis vēnit prīmus?
Vīdī amīcum tuum in ecclēsiā.

Equī in campō currēbant.
Ideae malae nōn vīcērunt.
De tē putābam.
Vīdimus fulmen.
Fluvius frīgidus erat.

Translation 6 (Vocabulary review)

Quis eum vīdit?
Hic cattus improbus est.
In sellā sedet.
Volō terrās incōgitātās invenīre.
Perdidimus clāvem.
Nox erat et caelus niger erat.
Mīlitēs in forō stant.
Perdidit fidem.
Amō Rōmam antīquam et Graeciam antīquam.
Dedērunt nōbīs dōnum splendidum.

Lesson IX

Ancient Romans didn't have sugar. Sugar was known only as a medicine from India. Instead of sugar Romans used honey.

Verbs
errō, errāre, errāvī, errātum (1) – to be wrong, to make a mistake
convincō, convincere, convīcī, convictum (3) – to convince
mittō, mittere, mīsī, missum (3) – to send, to throw, to shoot
explānō, explānāre, explānāvī, explānātum (1) – to explain
crēscō, crēscere, crēvī, crētum (3) – to grow
excūsō, excūsāre, excūsāvī, excūsātum (1) – to excuse, to be an excuse

MEL = HONEY

Nouns
futūrum, futūrī, n. (3) – future
in futūrō – in the future
palātium, palātiī, n. (2) – palace
amor, amōris, m. (3) – love
hiems, hiemis, f. (3) – winter
hieme – in winter
aestās, aestātis, f. (3) – summer
aestāte – in summer
annus, annī, m. (2) – year
proximō annō – next year
lūna, lūnae, f. (1) – moon
ad Lūnam – to the moon
poēma, poēmatis n. (3) – poem
arēna, arēnae, f. (1) – sand
rēgula, rēgulae, f. (1) – rule
cactus, cactī, m. (2) – cactus, thorny plant

Adjectives
proximus – next
sōlus – alone

Adverbs
crās – tomorrow
nunc – now
quŏque – also, too

CORVUS (RAVEN)

SĪMIA

Ancient Romans loved garlic!

ALLIUM

Make Sentences 1

Make sentences using antonyms. Example:
Hodiē trīstis sum. Crās laetus erō.
Today: *trīstis, discipulus, mīles, hic* (here)*, sōlus*
Tomorrow: *professor, dux, cum amīcīs, laetus, illic* (there)

Translation 1 (Future Imperfect tense – *esse*)
Future Imperfect tense is also known as the Simple Future tense.

She says that in the future she won't be lazy.
My father will be at home.
If we are alone, we won't be happy.
The soldiers will be on the square tomorrow.
The king will be in his palace.

Where will you be in summer?
God's love will be with you (plural) forever.
(in saecula saeculōrum)
In winter the ocean will be cold.
I will be with you next year.
Who will be with me?

Make Sentences 2 (Future Imperfect tense)

Make sentences using the Future Imperfect tense "I" form of the verbs *esse* and *discere:*
erō – I will be; *dīscam* – I will study
Example: **Romae erō, architectūram dīscam.** I will be in Rome, and I will study architecture.

Where you will be: *in insulā dēsertā; domi* – at home; *in ūniversitāte; in silvā; in Australiā; Novi Eboraci* – in New York City *(Novum Eboracum); Lutetiae* (*Lutetia* = Paris); *in Moscoviā; in navem* – on a ship

What you will study: *migrātiō cētōrum* – whale migration (Acc. Case: *migrātiōnem cētōrum*); *biologia; lingua avum* (bird language); *physica; theologia; astronomia; mathematica; lingua Anglica* – English; *lingua Francogallica* – French; *lingua Germanica* – German language; *lingua Russica* – Russian language

Did ancient Romans shake hands? Yes, although a handshake was not a casual greeting. It was used to confirm deals and agree treaties. This silver Roman coin from AD 97 shows a handshake.
Inscription: **Concordia exercituum** – Peace of / with the army
concordia, concordiae, f. (1) – agreement, peace, good relations
exercitus, exercitūs, m. (4) – army

Roman dinners usually started with an egg appetizer and ended with an apple dessert. That's why the Latin saying *ab ovo usque ad malum* – 'from the egg to the apple' means 'from the beginning to the end.'

Translation 2   (Future Imperfect tense)

Reminder:

1st and 2nd Conjugation verbs:

To form the Imperfect Future tense remove *-re* from the end of the infinitive of the verb and add the following endings:

I	*–bo*	we	*–bimus*
you (singular)	*–bis*	you (plural)	*–bitis*
he/she/it	*–bit*	they	*–bunt*

3rd and 4th Conjugation verbs:

To form the Imperfect Future tense remove *-ere* from the end of the infinitive of the verb and add the following endings:

I	*–am*	we	*–emus*
you (singular)	*–es*	you (plural)	*–etis*
he/she/it	*–et*	they	*–ent*

Use the Present and the Future forms of each verb in your translation.

Kids play today, and they will play tomorrow. *(lūdunt, lūdent)*

We say the truth today, and tomorrow we'll say the truth too. *(dīcēmus, dīcimus)*

A teacher teaches today, and he will teach tomorrow. *(docēbit, docet)*

A bird sings in summer and it will sing in winter. *(cantat, cantābit)*

A professor is writing his book now, and he will be writing his book next year. *(scrībit, scrībet)*

If you are wrong today, you will be wrong tomorrow. *(errābis, errās)*

I know nothing *(nihil)* now, but I will know everything *(omnia)* next year. *(sciō, sciam)*

Students read today, and they will read tomorrow too. *(legent, legunt)*

I want this now, and I will always want this. *(volō, volam)*

They don't convince us now, and they won't convince us in the future. *(convincunt, convincent)*

The motto of the British Isle of Man is:

Quocunque ieceris, stabit – Wherever you throw it, it will stand (reference to *triskele*, the 3-legged ancient Greek symbol that was adopted in Medieval Europe as a symbol of the Trinity)

iaciō, iacere, iēcī, iactum (3) – to throw, to cast

stō, stāre, stetī, statum (1) – to stand • *iēceris* – Future Perfect

stābit – Future Imperfect (Simple Future)

Make Sentences 3

Roman spoon, 4th-5th century

Use the command form of one verb, and the past participle of another verb from the set below.
Example: ***Scrībe epistulam! Epistula scrīpta est.*** Write a letter! The letter is written.

Actions: *scrībere – Scrībe! – scrīptus*
          edere – Ede! – ēsus

Objects:

epistula; cētus (whale); *liber; gelatum* (ice cream); *Historia regum Britanniae*
(The History of the Kings of Britain) – Acc. Case ***Historiam regum Britanniae***
mūs (mouse) – Acc. Case: ***murem;***
īnscrīptiō in marmōre (inscription on marble) – Acc. Case: ***īnscrīptiōnem in marmōre.***

Translation 3 (Past Participle)
Reminder: The Past Participle (neuter) is the 4th Principal Part of Latin verbs.
They decline (change forms) similar to the 1st and 2nd Declension adjectives.

The book has been read.
He is/was sent to the Moon.
The city is destroyed by the enemies. (*ab inimīcīs* [Ablative Case] = by the enemies)
The poem is written in the sand.
The word is/has been spoken.
The land is/has been captured.
Many stories are told about the goddess Diana.
Everything (*omnia*) is given to you (plural).
The key (*clāvis*) is thrown into the sea.
The rules are explained.

> Ancient Romans used spoons and knives, but forks were used only for serving. Bronze and iron forks broke easily. Silver was too expensive for everyday. Steel was reserved for swords and sewing needles.

Translation 4 (Vocabulary review)

One *(ūnum)* if by land, two *(duō)* if by sea.
By itself this rule is not difficult.
From today you will work with me.
Caesar said, "The die has been cast."
Caesar Augustus said, "The play is done. Applaud!"

This is an unwritten law in our homeland.
We'll be with you in spirit.
Cactuses/cacti grow in the desert.
I work in the kitchen.
Ignorance is no excuse.

Lesson IX   Answer Key

Translation 1 (Future Imperfect tense – *esse*)

Dīcit quod in futūrō pigra nōn erit.
Si sōlī erimus, laetī nōn erimus.
Mīlitēs in forō crās erunt.
Rēx in palātiō suō erit.
Ubi aestāte eris?
Amor Deī vōbīscum in saecula saeculōrum erit.
Hieme ōceanī frīgidī erunt.
Erō tēcum proximō annō.
Quis mēcum erit?

Translation 2 (Future Imperfect tense)

Līberī lūdunt hodiē, et lūdent crās.
Dīcimus vēritātem hodiē, et quōque dīcēmus vēritātem crās.
Magister docet hodiē, et docēbit crās.
Avis cantat aestāt, et cantābit hieme.
Professor scrībit librum suum nunc, et scrībet librum suum proximō annō.
Si errās hodiē, errābis crās.
Nunc sciō nihil, sed sciam omnia proximō annō.
Discipulī legunt hodiē, et quōque legent crās.
Nunc hoc volō, et hoc volam semper.
Nunc nōs nōn convincunt, et nōn convincent nōs in futūrō.

Translation 3 (Past Participle)

Liber lēctus est.
Ad Lūnam missus est.
Urbs ab inimīcīs dēlēta est.
Poēma in arēnā scrīptum est.
Verbum dictum est.

Terra capta est.
Multās fabulās de deā Diānā nārrātae sunt.
Omnia vōbīs data sunt.
Clāvis in marī iacta est.
Rēgulae explānātae sunt.

Translation 4 (Vocabulary review)

Unum, si per terram, duō si per mare.
Per sē, haec regula difficilis nōn est.
Ab hōc diē labōrābis mēcum.
Caesar dīxit, "Alea iacta est."
Caesar Augustus dīxit, "Acta est fabula. Plaudite."
Hoc est lēx nōn scrīpta in patriā nostrā.
Tēcum erimus in spīritū.
Cactī in dēsertō crēscunt.
In culīnā labōrō.
Ignōrantia nōn excūsat.

Lesson X

Verbs

cōnstruō, cōnstruere, cōnstrūxī, cōnstrūctum (3) – to build, to construct
lavō, lavāre, lāvī, lavātum / lautum (1) – wash
currō, currere, cucurrī, cursum (3) – to run.
exeō, exīre, exiī / exīvī, exitum (irregular) – to come out
gelō, gelāre, gelāvī, gelātum (1) – to freeze, to be chilled
pūgnō, pūgnāre, pūgnāvī, pūgnātum (1) – to fight

Nouns

oculus, oculī, m. (2) – eye
acta, actae, f. (3) – beach, coast
hērōs, hērōis, m. (3) – hero, demigod
bactērium, bactēriī, n. (2) – bacterium, bacteria
āēr, āeris, m. (3) – air
raeda, raedae, f. (1) – car, carriage
invidia, invidiae, f. (1) – envy
nāvis, nāvis, f. (3) – ship
gelātum, gelātī n. (2) – ice cream

OSTREA (OYSTER)

Adjectives

fīrmus – solid, firm • *sordidus* – dirty

Etymology – Word Origins
The English word 'noon' comes from the Latin *nōna hora* - the ninth hour. In ancient Rome the ninth hour was at 3 pm.

Translation 1 (Instrumental Ablative Case)

When talking about an 'instrument' with/by which something is done,
you can use the Ablative Case without any preposition. For example:
Scrībō pennā. = I write with a quill.
When an action is performed by a person, use the preposition *a* + Ablative Case = by:
Liber a magistrō scrīptus est = The book is written by a teacher.

I convince people with my words.
She sees this with her [own] eyes.
The road is/has been built by a king.
The dinner is/has been prepared by my mother.
The city is/was destroyed by the sea.

A wolf is/was captured by a shepherd.
He teaches with/by stories.
I wash the window with water.
We are liberated by the truth.
I work with my hands.

Etymology – Word Origins

What is the origin of the word TORPEDO? Surprisingly, it comes from the Latin verb *torpeō, torpēre, torpuī (2) – to be motionless, to be slow* **Torpēdō** in Latin means sluggishness, slowness. It is also the name of the stingray, the fish that defends itself by stunning its enemy with an electric discharge, making its prey motionless and disoriented. In the 18th century the word *torpēdō* was adopted as the name of an explosive device used to sink enemy ships.

Etymology – Word Origins

Many familiar English last names connected to occupations come from Latin:

Bailey – a castle wall <<< *bacula* = sticks, palisade, *baculum* = staff
Butler – a cup bearer <<< *butticula* = drinking cup
Carpenter – wood-worker <<< *carpentum* = a chariot, a carriage; *carpentarius* = chariot maker
Chamberlain – personal attendant to the king <<< *camera* = room, chamber
Chandler – candle maker <<< *candelarius* = candle maker (Medieval Latin)
Chapman – salesman <<< *caupō* = shopkeeper, salesman
Clark – a priest <<< *clericus* = priest (Medieval Latin)
Cooper – barrel-maker <<< *cūpa* = barrel, *cūparius* – barrel-maker
Garner – keeper of a grain storehouse <<< *grānum* = grain, seed
Palmer – a pilgrim who has returned from the Holy Land <<< *palmarius* = a pilgrim (Medieval Latin) <<< *palma* = palm tree <<< pilgrims often wore palm branches in commemoration of their trip to the Holy Land
Porter – castle gate keeper <<< *porta* = gate
Potter – maker of pots <<< *pōtus* = drink
Spenser – household manager <<< *dispēnsāre* = to manage, to distribute
Taylor – tailor <<< *taliare* = to cut, to split (Medieval Latin)
Usher – door keeper <<< *ostium* = door, entrance

Translation 2 (Adjectives – Comparative and Superlative degrees)

Reminder: There are different ways to introduce a comparison in Latin.
One of them is *quam* = than • *Dracō fortior quam leō est.* = A dragon is stronger than a lion.
Another way is to use the Ablative Case (the Ablative of Comparison) without *quam*:
Dracō fortior leōne est. = A dragon is stronger than a lion.

Choose the correct adjective: Comparative or Superlative degree.
A small city is better than a big city. *(feminine: melior / optima)*
Winter is good, but summer is the best. *(feminine: melior / optima)*
A dolphin *(delphīnus)* is big, but a whale *(cētus)* is bigger. (masculine: *maior / maximus*)
A bird is small, but an insect is smaller. (neuter: *minorius / minimum*)
Jupiter is the biggest planet. (feminine: *maior / maxima*)
This island is the farthest out. (feminine: *exterior / extrēma*)
Nerō was the worst emperor. (masculine: *pēior / pessimus*)
This is my last word. (neuter: *ulterius / ultimum*)
This book is short, but this story is shorter. (feminine: *brevior / brevissima*)

Translation 3 (Latin prepositions review 1)

Let's recall Latin prepositions and the cases they are used with:
in = in (location) + Ablative Case; *in* = into, to (direction) + Accusative Case
de = about, from + Ablative Case; *inter* = between, among + Accusative Case
e/ex = from, out of + Ablative Case; *cum* = with + Ablative Case
ā/ab = from, by + Ablative Case; *ad* = to, toward + Accusative Case
per = through, by + Accusative Case

On an empty tablet (*tabula rāsa*) nothing is written.
I go from the field to the beach.
Birds fly from tree to tree.
Who is looking out the window?
He tells us about the heroes of Ancient Greece
(*Graecia antīqua*)
She lives between the mountain and the river.

A lion is running toward the ocean.
They didn't come by land,
they came by the ocean.
We stand on solid ground. (*terra firma*)

Translation 4 (Latin prepositions review 2)

Fish live in water.
Caesar came to the river Rubicōn.
Do bacteria live in the dirty air?
Goddess Venus is/was born (*nāta est*) from the ocean.
Don't tell them about your car!
Enemies came to the gates of the city.
Soldiers come out of the gates.
He said that out of envy.
We were among friends.
The spaceship (*nāvis spatialis*) is going to the stars.

Translation 5 (Vocabulary review)

Friends go to the beach.
One ice cream per person!
The divine emperor is not smart/intelligent.
I fight with words, not with a sword.
Faith is a treasure.
Do you understand? I understand nothing!
Jupiter is the greatest god of the Romans.
I can help you.
Time reveals the truth.
The middle road is the best road.

Etymology – Word Origins
What is the origin of the word JOURNAL? JOURNAL comes from Latin *diurnus* = "daily" << *dies* = day

ĪNSULA = AN APARTMENT BUILDING

VĪLLA = A LARGE COUNTRY HOUSE

DOMUS = A TOWNHOUSE

URSUS

PORCUS

TESTŪDŌ

Lesson X   Answer Key

Translation 1   (Instrumental Ablative Case)

Convincō hominēs verbīs meīs.
Videt hoc oculīs suīs.
Via cōnstrūcta ā rēge est.
Cēna parāta ā mātre meā est.
Urbs marī dēlēta est.
Lupus ā pastōre captus est.
Docet fābulīs.
Lavō fenestram aquā.
Līberātī sumus vēritāte.
Labōrō manibus meīs.

Translation 2   (Adjectives – Comparative and Superlative degrees)

Urbs parva melior est quam urbs māgna.
Hiems bona, sed aestās optima est.
Delphīnus māgnus, sed cētus maior est.
Avīs parva, sed insectum minorius est.
Iuppiter planēta maxima est.
Haec īnsula extrēma est.
Nerō imperātor pessimus est.
Hoc est verbum ultimum meum.
Hic liber brevis, sed haec fabula brevior est.

Translation 3   (Latin prepositions review 1)

In tabulā rāsā nihil scrīptum est.   *Venī mēcum.*
Eō ā campō ad actam.   *Habitat inter montem et fluvium.*
Avēs volant ab arbōre ad arbōrem.   *Leō ad ōceanum currit.*
Or: Avēs volant ex arbōre in arbōrem.   *Nōn per terram, per ōceanum vēnērunt.*
Quis ex fenestrā spectat?   *Stāmus in terrā firmā.*
Nārrat nōbīs de hērōibus Graeciae antīquae.

Translation 4 (Latin prepositions review 2)

Piscēs in aquā habitant.
Caesar ad Rubicōnem fluvium vēnit.
Habitantne bacteria in āere sordidō?
Dea Venus ex ōceanō nāta est.
Nōlī eīs de raedā tuā dīcere!
Inimīcī ad portās urbis vēnērunt.
Mīlitēs ex portīs exeunt.
Hoc ex invidiā dīxit.
Inter amīcōs erāmus.
Nāvis spatialis ad stēllās it.

Translation 5 (Vocabulary review)

Amīcī ad actam eunt.
Unum gelātum per capita!
Imperātor dīvus intellegēns nōn est.
Pūgnō verbīs, nōn gladiō.
Fidēs thēsaurus est.
Intellegis? Nihil intellegō!
Iuppiter deus maximus Rōmānōrum est.
Possum tibi iuvāre.
Tempus vēritātem revēlat.
Via media optima est.

www.ingramcontent.com/pod-product-compliance
Lightning Source LLC
Chambersburg PA
CBHW041433010526
44118CB00002B/65